Collins

Easy Learning

GCSE Foundation

Maths

Exam Practice Workbook

FOR AQA B

Keith Gordon

Contents

Algebra

Statistical representation

1 Zeke did a survey of the number of passengers in some cars passing the school.

The results are shown in the table.

Number of passengers	Tally	Frequency
1	⊬⊬⊬ ⊬⊬⊬ ⊬⊬⊬ ⊬⊬⊬ /	21
2	⊬⊬⊬ ⊬⊬⊬ ///	
3		8
4	⊬⊬⊬ /	
5	//	

a Complete the frequency column.   [1 mark]

b Complete the tally column.   [1 mark]

c How many cars were surveyed altogether?

_____   [1 mark]

d Explain why the total number of passengers in all the cars was 105.

_____

_____ [2 marks]

2 The pictogram shows the number of letters delivered to a company during five days.

⊠ represents 20 letters.

Day		Number of letters
Monday	⊠ ⊠ ⊠ ▷	65
Tuesday	⊠ ⊠ ⊠ ⊠ ⊠	
Wednesday	⊠ ⊠ ⊠ ◺	
Thursday		40
Friday		35

a Complete the 'number of letters' column.   [1 mark]

b Complete the pictogram column.   [1 mark]

c How many letters were delivered altogether during the week?

_____   [1 mark]

This page tests you on   • statistics • collecting data • pictograms

1 This table shows the numbers of hours ten students spent watching TV and doing homework one weekend.

Student	A	B	C	D	E	F	G	H	I	J
Hours TV	2.5	1.5	4	3.5	5	1	3	4.5	3	2.5
Hours homework	1.5	3	1	1.5	0.5	2.5	1.5	0.5	2	1.5

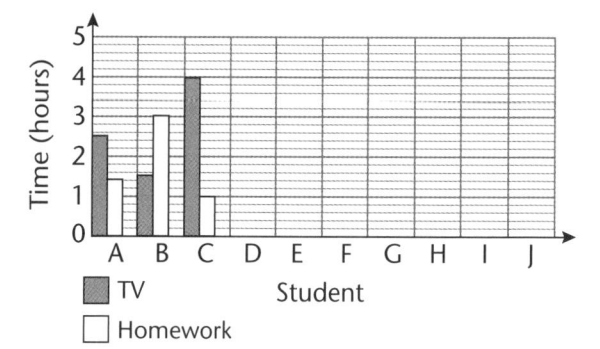

a Complete the dual bar chart to illustrate the data. **[2 marks]**

b The school recommends that students spend at least $1\frac{1}{2}$ hours doing homework each weekend. How many students did at least $1\frac{1}{2}$ hours homework?

_____ **[1 mark]**

c Bernice says that all the students spent more time watching TV than doing homework. Is this true? Explain your answer.

_____ **[1 mark]**

2 The line graph shows how the temperature in a greenhouse varies.

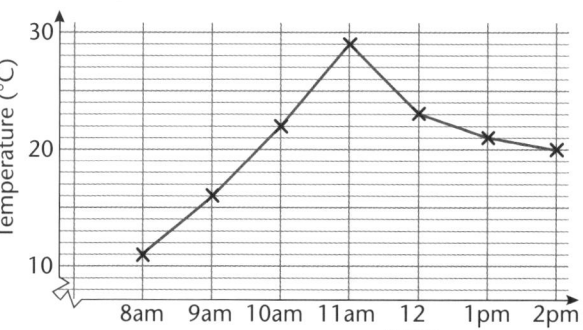

a What was the temperature at 9am? _____ °C **[1 mark]**

b During which hour did the temperature increase the most? _____ **[1 mark]**

c The gardener opened the ventilator to lower the temperature. At what time did he do this? _____ **[1 mark]**

d What was the approximate temperature at 10.30am? _____ °C **[1 mark]**

e Can you use the graph to predict the temperature at 6pm? Explain your answer.

_____ **[1 mark]**

This page tests you on • bar charts • line graphs

Averages

1 The table shows the numbers of passengers in some cars.

Number of passengers	Frequency
1	23
2	15
3	5
4	4
5	3

a How many cars were in the survey?

_____ **[1 mark]**

b What is the modal number of passengers per car?

_____ **[1 mark]**

c What is the median number of passengers per car?

_____ **[1 mark]**

d Cars with two or more passengers can use a 'car pool' lane on the motorway. What percentage of these cars could use the car pool lane?

_____ **[1 mark]**

2 a For the data 51, 74, 53, 74, 76, 58, 68, 51, 70 and 65 work out:

  i the mean

_____ **[1 mark]**

  ii the range

_____ **[1 mark]**

b A football team of 11 players has a mean weight of 84 kg.

  i How much do the 11 players weigh altogether?

_____ **[1 mark]**

  ii When the three substitutes are included, the 14 players have a mean weight of 87 kg. What is the mean weight of the three substitutes?

_____ **[2 marks]**

This page tests you on • mode • median • mean

F

1 The bar chart shows the numbers of spoonfuls of sugar that a group of workmen take in their morning tea.

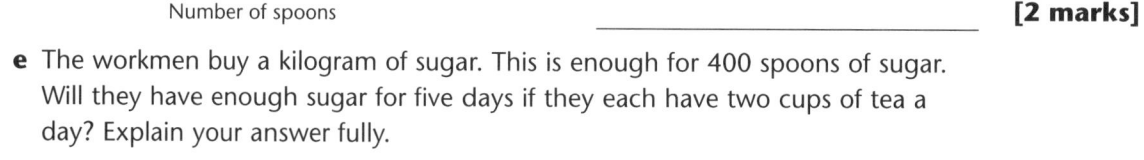

a How many workmen are there?

_____ **[1 mark]**

b What is the modal number of spoons?

_____ **[1 mark]**

c What is the median number of spoons?

_____ **[1 mark]**

d What is the mean number of spoons?

_____ **[2 marks]**

e The workmen buy a kilogram of sugar. This is enough for 400 spoons of sugar. Will they have enough sugar for five days if they each have two cups of tea a day? Explain your answer fully.

_____ **[1 mark]**

D

2 Ten workmates went ten-pin bowling.

a Their scores for the first game were: 87 123 121 103 93 231 145 46 65 46
Work out:

i the modal score _____ **[1 mark]**

ii the median score _____ **[1 mark]**

iii the mean score. _____ **[1 mark]**

b i Explain why the mode would not be a good average to use.

_____ **[1 mark]**

ii Explain why the mean would not be a good average to use.

_____ **[1 mark]**

c In the second game, the modal score was 105. Does this mean the players increased their overall scores? Explain your answer.

_____ **[1 mark]**

d In the third game, the mean was 120.

i Does this mean the players increased their overall scores? Explain your answer.

_____ **[1 mark]**

ii Can you tell whether the median for the third game was higher or lower than for the first game? Explain your answer.

_____ **[1 mark]**

This page tests you on • range • which average to use

Arranging data

1 The table shows the number of cars per house on a housing estate of 100 houses.

Number of cars	Number of houses
0	8
1	23
2	52
3	15
4	2

Work out:

a the modal number of cars

_____ [1 mark]

b the median number of cars

_____ [1 mark]

c the mean number of cars.

_____ [2 marks]

D

2 The table shows the scores of 200 boys in a mathematics exam.

The frequency polygon shows the scores of 200 girls in the same examination.

Mark, x	Frequency, f
$40 < x \leqslant 50$	27
$50 < x \leqslant 60$	39
$60 < x \leqslant 70$	78
$70 < x \leqslant 80$	31
$80 < x \leqslant 90$	13
$90 < x \leqslant 100$	12

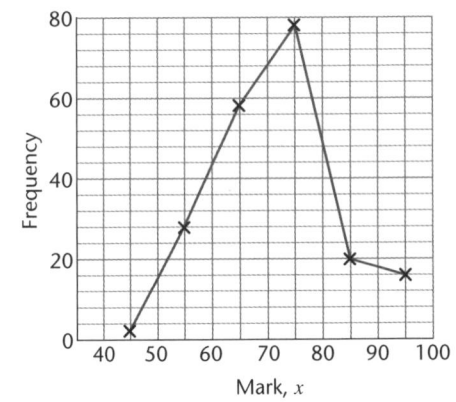

a Work out the mean mark for the boys' scores.

_____ [2 marks]

b On the same graph as the girls frequency polygon, draw the frequency polygon for the boys' scores. [1 mark]

c Who did better in the test, the boys or the girls? Give reasons for your answer.

_____

_____ [1 mark]

C

This page tests you on • frequency tables • grouped data

D

1 These are the weights of 20 guinea pigs, in grams, rounded to the nearest 10 grams.

130   90   220   210   190   130   160   110   230   90

80   120   130   240   180   150   70   220   240   130

a Using the key 1 | 3 to represent 130 grams, put the data into the stem-and-leaf diagram.

0 |
1 |
2 |

[2 marks]

Key 1 | 3 represents 130 grams

b Using the stem-and-leaf diagram, or otherwise, write down:

i the modal weight

_____ grams   **[1 mark]**

ii the median weight

_____ grams   **[1 mark]**

iii the range of the weights.

_____ grams   **[1 mark]**

C

2 A teacher recorded how many times her students were late during a term.

The stem-and-leaf diagram shows the data.

12 students were **never late**.

0 | 2   3   4   4   5   6   7
1 | 3   5   8   9   9
2 | 0   1   4   5
3 | 2
5 | 1

Key 1 | 7 represents 17 times late

a How many students there are in the form altogether?

_____   **[1 mark]**

b Work out the mean number of times late for the whole form.

_____   **[2 marks]**

This page tests you on   • **stem-and-leaf diagrams**

9

Probability

1 a State whether each of the following events is *impossible, very unlikely, unlikely, evens, likely, very likely* or *certain*.

   i you walking on the moon tomorrow

   _____ **[1 mark]**

   ii getting a six when a regular dice is thrown

   _____ **[1 mark]**

   iii tossing a coin and scoring a head

   _____ **[1 mark]**

   iv someone in the class going abroad for their holidays

   _____ **[1 mark]**

b On the probability scale, put a numbered arrow to show approximately the probability of each of the following outcomes of events happening.

$$0 \qquad\qquad\qquad \frac{1}{2} \qquad\qquad\qquad 1$$

   i The next car you see driving down the road will only have the driver inside. **[1 mark]**
   ii Someone in the class had porridge for breakfast. **[1 mark]**
   iii Picking a red card from a well shuffled pack of cards. **[1 mark]**
   iv Throwing a number less than seven with a regular dice. **[1 mark]**

2 A bag contains 20 coloured balls. Twelve are red, five are blue and the rest are white. A ball is taken from the bag at random.

a What is the probability that the ball is:

   i red

   _____ **[1 mark]**

   ii pink

   _____ **[1 mark]**

   iii blue or white?

   _____ **[1 mark]**

b Some more white balls are added to the bag so that the probability of getting a red ball is now $\frac{1}{2}$. How many red balls were added?

   _____ **[1 mark]**

G

E

This page tests you on   • the probability scale   • calculating probabilities

E

1 The probability that a milkman delivers the wrong sort of milk to a house is $\frac{3}{50}$.

a What is the probability that he delivers the correct sort of milk to a house?

_____ [1 mark]

b He delivers milk to 500 houses a day. Estimate the number of houses that get the wrong milk.

_____ [1 mark]

E

2 There are 900 squares on a 'Treasure map' at the school Summer Fayre.

One of the squares contains the treasure.

The Rogers decide to buy some squares.

Mr Rogers buys five squares, Mrs Rogers buys ten squares and their two children, Amy and Ben, buy two squares each.

a Which member of the family has the best chance of winning?
Explain your answer.

_____ [1 mark]

b What is the probability that Mr Rogers wins the treasure?

_____ [1 mark]

c What is the probability that one of the children wins the treasure?

_____ [1 mark]

d If the family put all their squares together, what is the probability that they will win the treasure?

_____ [1 mark]

C

3 John makes a dice and weights one side with a piece of sticky gum. He throws it 120 times. The table shows the results.

Score	1	2	3	4	5	6
Frequency	18	7	22	21	35	17
Relative frequency						

a Fill in the relative frequency row. Give your answers to 2 decimal places. **[2 marks]**

b Which side did John stick the gum on? Explain how you can tell.

_____ [1 mark]

This page tests you on
- probability of 'not' an event
- addition rule for mutually exclusive outcomes
- relative frequency

1 Pete's Café has a breakfast deal.

Three-item breakfast! Only £1		
Choose one of:	**Choose one of:**	**Choose one of:**
sausage or bacon	egg or hash browns	beans or toast

a There are eight possible 'three-item breakfast' combinations, for example, **sausage**, **egg**, **beans** or **sausage**, **egg**, **toast**.

List all the other possible combinations.

_____   _____

_____   _____

_____   _____

_____   _____   **[2 marks]**

b Fred tells his friend, 'I'll have what you are having.'

What is the probability that Fred gets bacon and eggs with his breakfast?

_____   **[1 mark]**

E

2 The sample space diagram shows the outcomes when a coin and a regular dice are thrown at the same time.

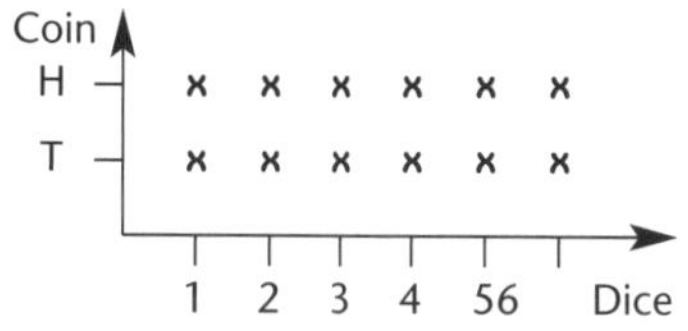

Coin
H – × × × × × ×
T – × × × × × ×

1 2 3 4 56 Dice

a How many possible outcomes are there when a coin and a dice are thrown together?

_____   **[1 mark]**

b When a coin and a dice are thrown together what is the probability that:

i the coin shows tails and the dice shows an even number

_____   **[1 mark]**

ii the coin shows heads and the dice shows a square number?

_____   **[1 mark]**

c Alicia and Zeek play a game with the coin and dice. If the coin lands on a head the score on the dice is doubled. If the coin lands on a tail 1 is subtracted from the score on the dice.

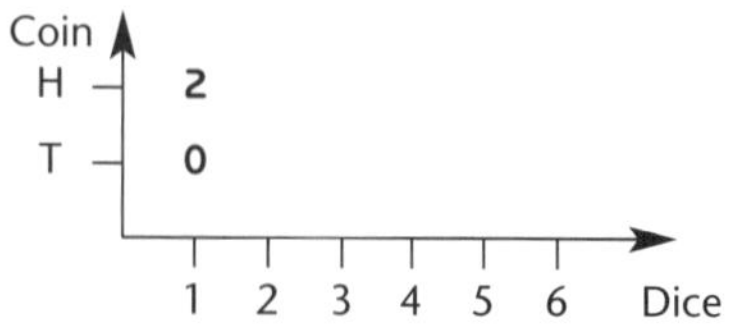

Coin
H – 2
T – 0

1 2 3 4 5 6 Dice

i Complete the sample space diagram to show all possible scores.   **[2 marks]**

ii What is the probability of an odd score?

_____   **[1 mark]**

D

This page tests you on   • **combined events**

12

C

1 A bag contains 30 balls that are either red or white. The ratio of red balls to white balls is 2 : 3.

a Zoe says that the probability of picking a red ball at random from the bag is $\frac{2}{3}$.

Explain why Zoe is wrong.

_____

_____ **[1 mark]**

b How many red balls are there in the bag?

_____ **[1 mark]**

c A ball is taken from the bag at random, its colour noted and then it is replaced.

This is done 200 times. How many of the balls would you expect to be red?

_____ **[1 mark]**

E

2 The two-way table shows the numbers of male and female teachers in four school departments.

	Male	**Female**
Mathematics	7	5
Science	11	7
RE	1	3
PE	3	3

a How many male teachers are there altogether?

_____ **[1 mark]**

b Which subject has equal numbers of male and female teachers?

_____ **[1 mark]**

c Nuna says that science is a more popular subject than mathematics for female teachers.

Explain why Nuna is wrong.

_____

_____ **[1 mark]**

d What is the probability that a teacher chosen at random from the table will be a female teacher of mathematics or science?

_____

_____ **[1 mark]**

This page tests you on • expectation • two-way tables

Pie charts

1 The table shows the results of a survey of 60 students, to find out what they do for lunch.

Lunch arrangement	Frequency	Angle
Use canteen	22	
Have sandwiches	18	
Go home	12	
Go to shopping centre	8	

Tom is going to draw a pie chart to show the data.

a Complete the column for the angle for each sector. **[2 marks]**

b Draw a fully labelled pie chart below.

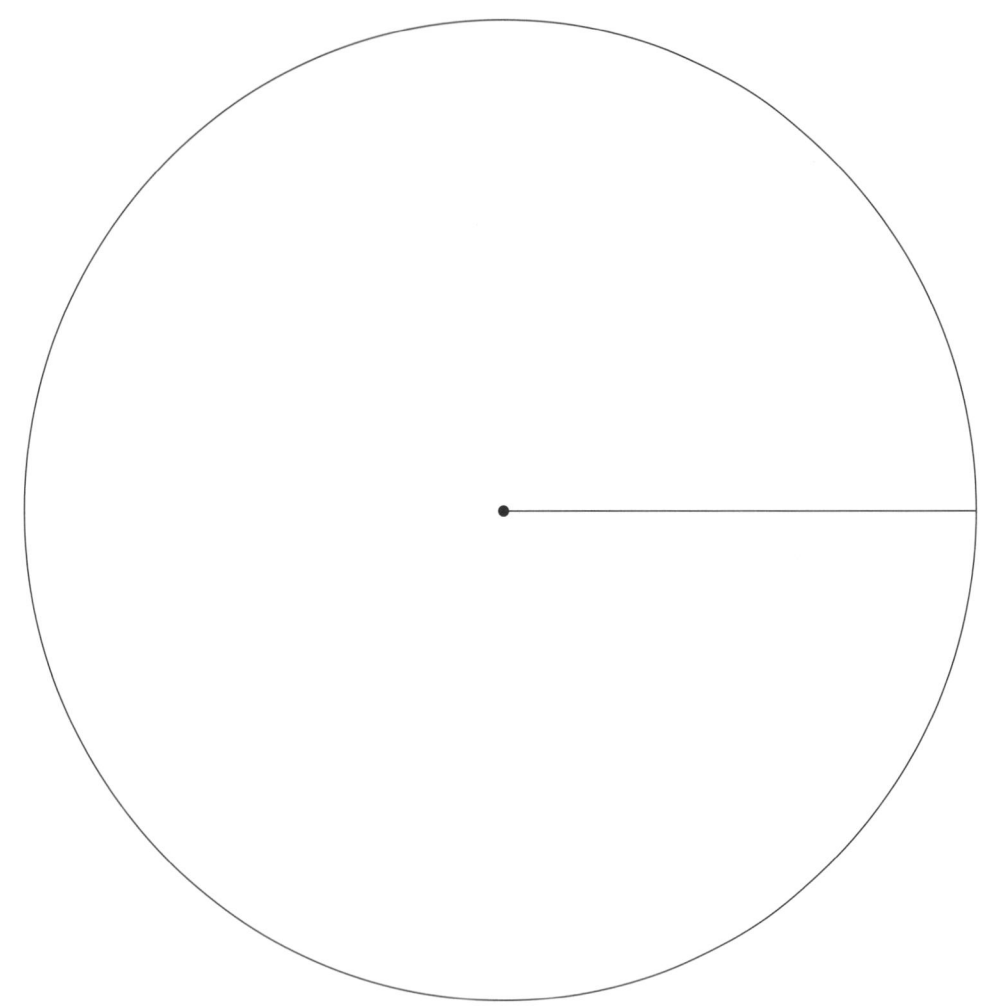

[2 marks]

c There are 1200 students in the school.

Estimate how many of them go to the shopping centre at lunchtime.

_____ **[1 mark]**

Scatter diagrams

1 A delivery driver records the distances and times for deliveries.

The table shows the results.

Delivery	Distance (km)	Time (minutes)
A	12	30
B	16	42
C	20	55
D	8	15
E	18	40
F	25	60
G	9	45
H	15	32
I	20	20
J	14	35

a Plot the values on the scatter diagram.

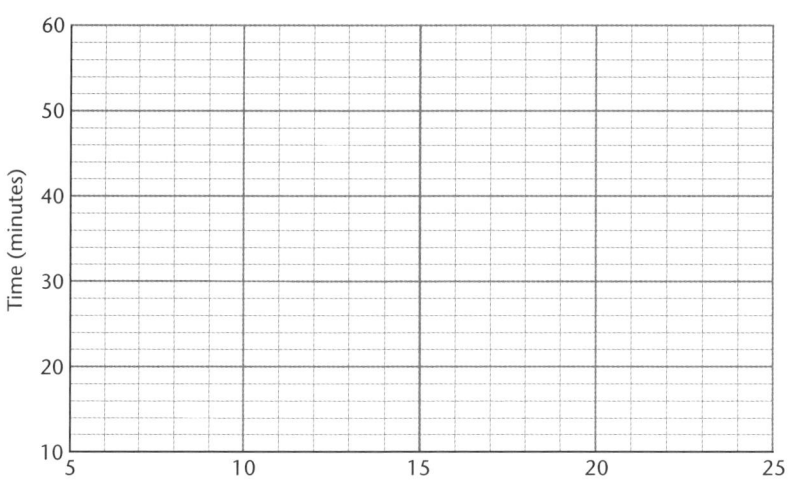

[2 marks]

b i During one of the deliveries the driver was stuck in a traffic jam.
Which delivery was this?

_____ [1 mark]

ii One of the deliveries was done very early in the morning when there was
no traffic. Which delivery was this?

_____ [1 mark]

c Ignoring the two values in **b**, draw a line of best fit through the rest of
the data. [1 mark]

d Under normal conditions, how long would you expect a delivery of 22 kilometres
to take?

_____ [1 mark]

This page tests you on • scatter diagrams • correlation • line of best fit

Surveys

1 Danny wanted to investigate the hypothesis:

> *Girls spend more time on mathematics coursework than boys do*.

a Design a two-way table that will help Danny collect data.

[2 marks]

b Danny collected data from 30 boys and 10 girls.

He found that, on average, the boys spent 10 hours and the girls spent 11 hours on their mathematics coursework.

Does this prove the hypothesis? Give reasons for your answer.

_____ **[1 mark]**

D

2 This graph shows the price index of petrol from 2000 to 2007. In 2000 the price of a litre of petrol was 60p.

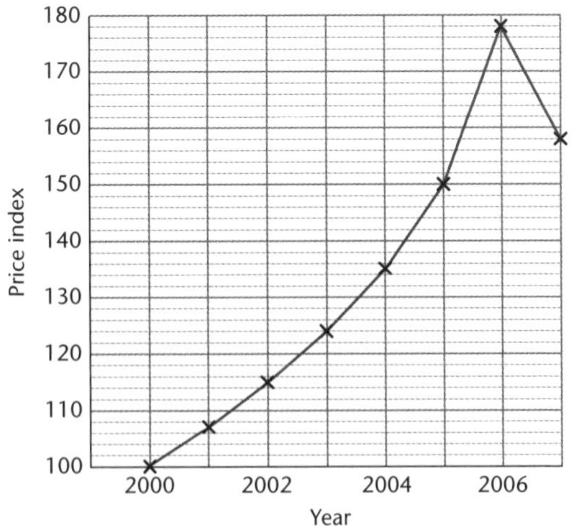

a Use the graph to estimate the price of a litre of petrol in 2007.

_____ **[1 mark]**

b A war in Iraq caused an oil crisis. Which year do you think this happened?

Explain how you can tell.

_____

_____

_____ **[1 mark]**

c Over the same period, the index for the cost of living rose by 38%.

Is the cost of petrol increasing faster or more slowly than the cost of living?

Explain your answer.

_____ **[1 mark]**

C

This page tests you on • surveys • social statistics

Handling data checklist

I can...

☐ draw and read information from bar charts, dual bar charts and pictograms

☐ find the mode and median of a list of data

☐ understand basic terms such as 'certain', 'impossible', 'likely'

You are working at (Grade G) level.

☐ work out the total frequency from a frequency table and compare data in bar charts

☐ find the range of a set of data

☐ find the mean of a set of data

☐ understand that the probability scale runs from 0 to 1

☐ calculate the probability of events with equally likely outcomes

☐ interpret a simple pie chart

You are working at (Grade F) level.

☐ read information from a stem-and-leaf diagram

☐ find the mode, median and range from a stem-and-leaf diagram

☐ list all the outcomes of two independent events and calculate probabilities from lists or tables

☐ calculate the probability of an event not happening when the probability of it happening is known

☐ draw a pie chart

You are working at (Grade E) level.

☐ draw an ordered stem-and-leaf diagram

☐ find the mean of a frequency table of discrete data

☐ find the mean from a stem-and-leaf diagram

☐ predict the expected number of outcomes of an event

☐ draw a line of best fit on a scatter diagram

☐ recognise the different types of correlation

☐ design a data collection sheet

☐ draw a frequency polygon for discrete data

You are working at (Grade D) level.

☐ find an estimate of the mean from a grouped table of continuous data

☐ draw a frequency diagram for continuous data

☐ calculate the relative frequency of an event from experimental data

☐ interpret a scatter diagram

☐ use a line of best fit to predict values

☐ design and criticise questions for questionnaires.

You are working at (Grade C) level.

Basic number

1 a Write down the answer to each calculation.

   i 8×9

                            _____ **[1 mark]**

   ii 40×7

                            _____ **[1 mark]**

   iii $240 \div 3$

                            _____ **[1 mark]**

b George has four cards with a number written on each of them.

   i He uses the cards to make a multiplication statement.

 $\times$  $=$

   What is the multiplication statement?

                            _____ **[1 mark]**

   ii He uses the cards to make a division statement.

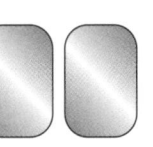 $\div$  $=$

   What is the division statement?

                            _____ **[1 mark]**

G

2 Two students work out the following calculation:

$2 + 4^2 \div 8$

Sammi gets an answer of 2.25. Ross gets an answer of 4.5.

Both of these answers are wrong.

a What is the answer to $2 + 4^2 \div 8$?

                            _____ **[1 mark]**

b Put brackets in the following calculations to make them true.

   i $2 + 4^2 \div 8 = 2.25$ **[1 mark]**

   ii $2 + 4^2 \div 8 = 4.5$ **[1 mark]**

D

This page tests you on   • times tables • order of operations and BODMAS

G

1 Work these out.

   a   2 5 7 6

      + 1 0 8 3

      _____

   b   1 2 9

      + 6 7 3 5

      _____

   c 78 + 2054 – 362

      _____   **[1 mark each]**

G

2 a When England won the world cup at Wembley in 1964 the attendance was given as 96 924.

   i Write 96 924 in words.

   _____   **[1 mark]**

   ii Round 96 924 to the nearest 100.   _____   **[1 mark]**

   iii Round 96 924 to the nearest 1000.   _____   **[1 mark]**

 b When Italy won the world cup in Berlin in 2006, the attendance was given as 69 000 rounded to the nearest hundred.

   i What is the value of the digit 9 in 69 000?   _____   **[1 mark]**

   ii What is the smallest value the attendance could have been?   _____   **[1 mark]**

   iii What is the largest value the attendance could have been?   _____   **[1 mark]**

   iv About one third of the spectators were Italian.

   Approximately how many spectators were Italian?   _____   **[1 mark]**

F

3 Work these out.

   a   3 0 7 6

      – 2 1 7 8

      _____

   b   6 9 0 3

      – 3 7 2 5

      _____

   c 86 + 1623 – 484

      _____   **[1 mark each]**

F

4 Farmer Bill has 1728 sheep on his farm. Farmer Jill has 589 sheep on her farm.

 a How many more sheep does farmer Bill have than farmer Jill?

   _____   **[1 mark]**

 b Farmer Jill sells all of her sheep to farmer Bill. How many does he have now?

   _____   **[1 mark]**

This page tests you on
- place value • rounding
- **column addition and subtraction**

1 Work these out.

   a   7 6

      $\times$ 4

     _____

   b   6)156

   c 54 $\times$ 7

   d 384 $\div$ 8

_____ _____ **[1 mark each]**

G

2 a Mary buys four cans of cola at 68p per can.

   i How much do the four cans cost altogether?

_____ **[1 mark]**

   ii She pays with a £5 note. How much change does she get?

_____ **[1 mark]**

  b In the school hall, there are 24 chairs in each row.

   There are 30 rows of chairs.

   How many chairs are there in total?

_____ **[1 mark]**

  c Year 10 has 196 students in seven forms.

   Each form has the same number of students.

   How many students are there in each form?

_____ **[1 mark]**

G

3 Show the calculation you need to do to work out each answer.

Then calculate the answer.

  a How much change do I get from £20 if I spend £12.85?

_____

_____ **[1 mark]**

  b I buy three ties at a total cost of £14.55. What is the price of each tie?

_____

_____ **[1 mark]**

  c Cartons of eggs contain 12 eggs. How many eggs will there be in nine cartons?

_____

_____ **[1 mark]**

F

This page tests you on   • multiplying and dividing by single-digit numbers
  • problems in words

Fractions

G

1 a Which two of these fractions are equivalent to $\frac{3}{4}$?

$\frac{9}{12}$ $\frac{6}{7}$ $\frac{8}{20}$ $\frac{60}{80}$

_____ and _____   **[1 mark]**

b Shade $\frac{3}{4}$ of this shape.

[1 mark]

c i What fraction of this shape is shaded?

_____   **[1 mark]**

ii What fraction is not shaded?

_____   **[1 mark]**

F

2 a i Shade $\frac{2}{9}$ of this shape.

[1 mark]

ii Shade $\frac{1}{3}$ of this shape.

[1 mark]

b Use your answer to part (a) to write down the answer to:

$\frac{2}{9} + \frac{1}{3} =$

_____   **[1 mark]**

F

3 The ratio of grey squares to white squares in this shape is $2:3$.

a Zoe says, 'That means the grey squares must be $\frac{2}{3}$ of the shape.'

Explain why Zoe is wrong.

_____   **[1 mark]**

b Write down **two** other fractions that are equivalent to $\frac{2}{5}$.

_____ and _____   **[1 mark]**

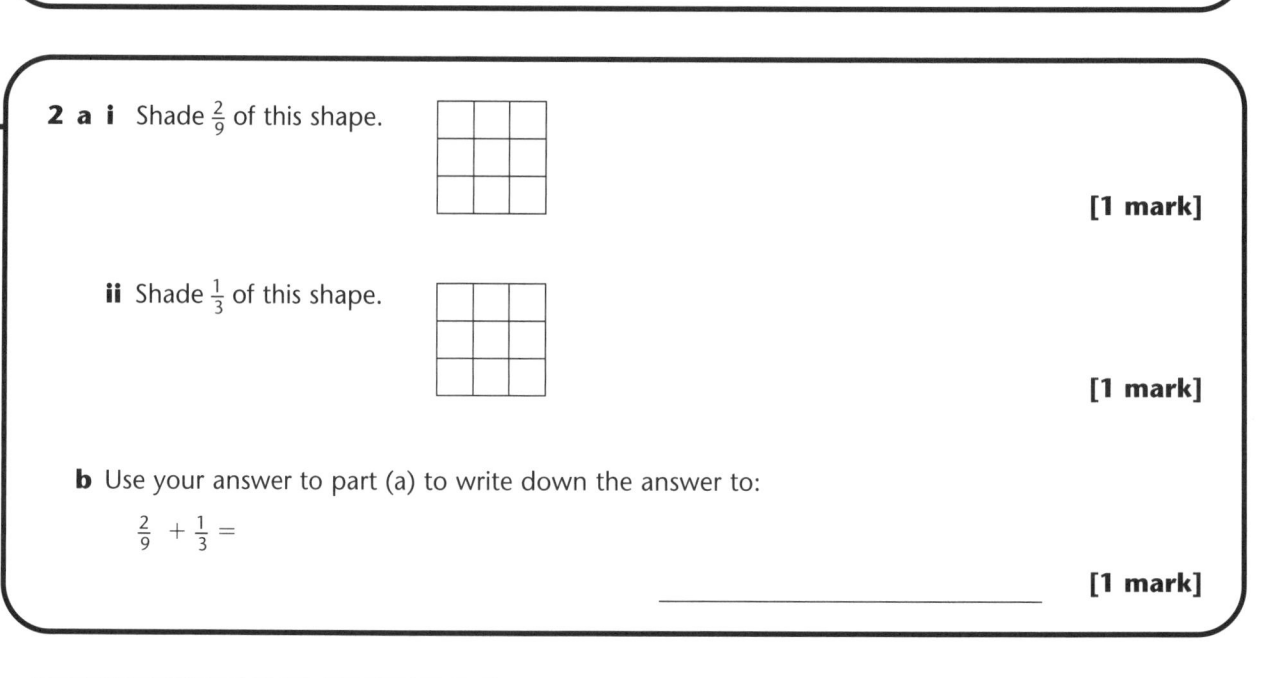

This page tests you on
- fractions of a shape
- adding and subtracting simple fractions
- equivalent fractions

G

1 a Shade squares in each of these diagrams so that $\frac{1}{4}$ of each diagram is shaded.

i

ii

iii

iv

[2 marks]

b Fill in the boxes to make the following fractions equivalent.

i $\frac{3}{7} = \frac{\square}{28}$

ii $\frac{5}{8} = \frac{20}{\square}$

iii $\frac{15}{18} = \frac{5}{\square}$

iv $\frac{\square}{3} = \frac{16}{24}$

[1 mark each]

c Cancel the following fractions, giving each answer in its simplest form.

i $\frac{16}{28} =$ _____

ii $\frac{9}{15} =$ _____

iii $\frac{12}{30} =$ _____

iv $\frac{21}{28} =$ _____

[1 mark each]

d Put the following fractions in order, with the smallest first.

$\frac{7}{10}$ $\frac{4}{5}$ $\frac{13}{20}$

_____ [1 mark]

F

2 a Change the following top-heavy fractions into mixed numbers.

i $\frac{9}{5} =$ _____

ii $\frac{17}{7} =$ _____

iii $\frac{21}{8} =$ _____

iv $\frac{31}{4} =$ _____

[1 mark each]

b Change the following mixed numbers into top-heavy fractions.

i $1\frac{6}{11} =$ _____

ii $1\frac{3}{8} =$ _____

iii $2\frac{1}{3} =$ _____

iv $4\frac{3}{5} =$ _____

[1 mark each]

This page tests you on
• equivalent fractions and cancelling
• top-heavy fractions and mixed numbers

E

1 a Fill in the boxes to make the following fractions equivalent.

i $\frac{3}{10} = \frac{\square}{20}$ **ii** $\frac{5}{8} = \frac{\square}{16}$ **iii** $\frac{1}{3} = \frac{\square}{6}$ **iv** $\frac{3}{4} = \frac{\square}{12}$ **[1 mark each]**

b Use the answers to part **a** to work these out.

Cancel the answer to its simplest form.

i $\frac{1}{20} + \frac{3}{10}$ _____ **[1 mark]**

ii $\frac{3}{16} + \frac{5}{8}$ _____ **[1 mark]**

iii $\frac{1}{6} + \frac{1}{3}$ _____ **[1 mark]**

iv $\frac{1}{12} + \frac{3}{4}$ _____ **[1 mark]**

c Use the answers to part **a** to work these out.

Cancel the answer to its simplest form.

i $\frac{17}{20} - \frac{3}{10}$ _____ **[1 mark]**

ii $\frac{15}{16} - \frac{5}{8}$ _____ **[1 mark]**

iii $\frac{5}{6} - \frac{1}{3}$ _____ **[1 mark]**

iv $\frac{11}{12} - \frac{3}{4}$ _____ **[1 mark]**

F

2 a On MacDonald's Farm there are a total of 245 hectares.

$\frac{2}{5}$ of the land is planted for crops, the rest is used for animals.

i What fraction of the land is used for animals?

_____ **[1 mark]**

ii How many hectares are used for crops?

_____ **[1 mark]**

b MacDonald has 120 sheep.

$\frac{3}{4}$ of the sheep each gives birth to two lambs, the rest give birth to one lamb.

How many lambs are born altogether?

_____ **[2 marks]**

c MacDonald has 220 cows. He sells $\frac{1}{4}$ of them.

How many cows has he got left after that?

_____ **[2 marks]**

This page tests you on
- adding and subtracting fractions
- finding a fraction of a quantity

1 a Work these out, giving each answer in its simplest form.

    i $\frac{2}{3} \times \frac{6}{11}$ _____ [1 mark]

    ii $\frac{3}{8} \times \frac{4}{9}$ _____ [1 mark]

    iii $\frac{5}{6} \times \frac{3}{20}$ _____ [1 mark]

    iv $\frac{9}{10} \times \frac{5}{6}$ _____ [1 mark]

b Work out each of these and give the answer as a mixed number in its simplest form.

    i $4 \times \frac{3}{8}$ _____ [1 mark]

    ii $5 \times \frac{3}{10}$ _____ [1 mark]

    iii $6 \times \frac{1}{3}$ _____ [1 mark]

    iv $8 \times \frac{3}{4}$ _____ [1 mark]

E

2 a In a school there are 1500 students. 250 of the students are in Year 7.

What fraction of the students are in Year 7?

_____ [2 marks]

b There are 120 girls in Year 7. 40 of the girls are left-handed.

What fraction of the girls are left-handed?

_____ [2 marks]

E

3 a Frank earns £18 000 per year. He pays $\frac{3}{20}$ of his pay in tax.

How much tax does he pay?

_____ [2 marks]

b Packets of washing powder normally contain 1.2 kg.

A special offer pack contains $\frac{1}{6}$ more than a normal pack.

How much does the special offer pack contain?

_____ [2 marks]

E

This page tests you on
- multiplying fractions
- one quantity as a fraction of another
- problems in words

Rational numbers and reciprocals

D

1 a Write each fraction as a decimal. Give the answer as a terminating decimal
or a recurring decimal as appropriate.

i $\frac{7}{40}$ _____ [1 mark]

ii $\frac{11}{15}$ _____ [1 mark]

iii $\frac{5}{6}$ _____ [1 mark]

iv $\frac{9}{50}$ _____ [1 mark]

b $\frac{1}{9} = 0.1111...$ $\frac{2}{9} = 0.2222...$
Use this information to write down:

i $\frac{4}{9}$ _____ [1 mark]

ii $\frac{5}{9}$ _____ [1 mark]

c $\frac{1}{11} = 0.0909...$ $\frac{2}{11} = 0.1818...$
Use this information to write down:

i $\frac{3}{11}$ _____ [1 mark]

ii $\frac{6}{11}$ _____ [1 mark]

C

2 a Write down the reciprocal of each of these numbers.
Give your answer as a fraction or a mixed number.

i 10 _____ [1 mark]

ii $\frac{3}{4}$ _____ [1 mark]

b Write each of the answers to **a** as a terminating or a recurring decimal.

i _____ [1 mark]

ii _____ [1 mark]

c Work out the reciprocal of each number.

i 1.25 _____ [1 mark]

ii 2.5 _____ [1 mark]

iii 5 _____ [1 mark]

d The sequence 1.25, 2.5, 5, 10, ... is formed by doubling each term to find
the next term.

Using your answer to part **c**, explain how you know the reciprocal of 40
is 0.025 without doing the calculation $1 \div 40$.

_____

_____ [2 marks]

This page tests you on
- rational numbers
- converting terminating decimals into fractions
- finding reciprocals

Negative numbers

1 These maps show the maximum and minimum temperatures in five towns during a six-month period.

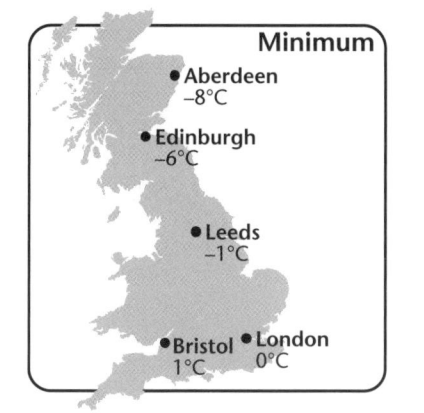
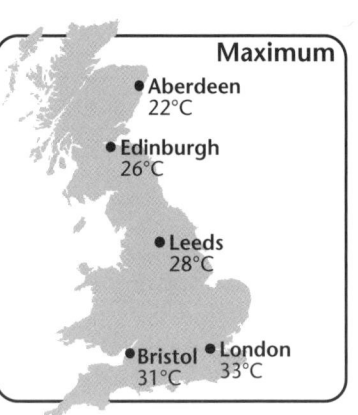

a Which town had the lowest minimum temperature?

_____ **[1 mark]**

b What is the difference between the lowest and highest **minimum** temperatures?

_____ **[1 mark]**

c Which two towns had a difference of 30 degrees between the maximum and minimum temperatures?

_____ **[1 mark]**

d Which town had the greatest difference between the maximum and minimum temperatures?

_____ **[1 mark]**

2 a The number line has the value −2.2 marked on it.

−2.2
↓

| | | | | | | |
|−3|−2|−1|0|1|2|3|

Mark the following values on the number line.

i −1.4 **ii** 1.7 **iii** −0.3 **[2 marks]**

b Fill in the missing values on this number line.

[ ] [ ] [ ] −1.9 −1.8 −1.7

[1 mark]

c What number is halfway between:

i −4 and 8 **ii** −11 and −8?

_____ _____ **[1 mark each]**

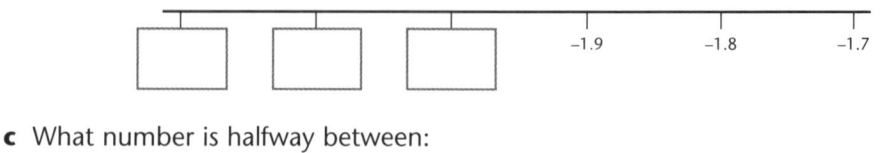

This page tests you on • negative numbers • the number line

1 Look at the following number cards.

a What is the total of the numbers on all the cards?

_____ **[1 mark]**

b Which two cards will make this calculation true?

 + 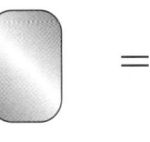 =

_____ and _____ **[1 mark]**

c i Which card would make the answer to this calculation as small as possible?

 −  =

_____ **[1 mark]**

ii What is the smallest possible answer?

_____ **[1 mark]**

d i Which card would make the answer to this calculation as large as possible?

 −  =

_____ **[1 mark]**

ii What is the largest possible answer?

_____ **[1 mark]**

2 In this magic square the numbers in each row, column and diagonal add up to the same total.

Fill in the missing numbers.

3		
−3		
−6	7	−7

[2 marks]

This page tests you on • addition and subtraction with negative numbers

More about number

1 Here are six number cards.

| 6 | 7 | 10 | 11 | 12 | 13 |

F

a Which **two** of the numbers are multiples of 3?

_____ [1 mark]

b Which **two** of the numbers are factors of 30?

_____ [1 mark]

c In this magic square the numbers in each row, column and diagonal add up to the same total. Use numbers from the cards above to complete the magic square.

		8
5	9	

[2 marks]

2 a Write down the factors of each number.

i 33

_____ [1 mark]

ii 18

_____ [1 mark]

b From this list of numbers:

84, 85, 86, 88, 89, 90

write down:

i a multiple of 3

_____ [1 mark]

ii a multiple of 5.

_____ [1 mark]

c Counter A counts a beat every 3 seconds.

Counter B counts a beat every 4 seconds

Counter C counts a beat every 5 seconds.

They all start at the same time.

After how many seconds will all three counters next count a beat at the same time?

_____ [1 mark]

C

This page tests you on   • multiples • factors

Primes and squares

D

1 Here are seven number cards.

| 6 | 9 | 10 | 11 | 13 | 15 | 16 |

a Which **two** of the numbers are prime numbers?

_____ [1 mark]

b Jen says that all prime numbers are odd.

Give an example to show that Jen is wrong.

_____ [1 mark]

c Which **two** of the numbers are square numbers?

_____ [1 mark]

d Ken says that all square numbers end in the digits 1, 4, 6 or 9.

Give an example to show that Ken is wrong.

_____ [1 mark]

e Which **two** of the cards will give a result that is a prime number in the calculation below?

| 6 | $+$ | | $=$ | prime |

_____ [2 marks]

D

2 P is a prime number. S is a square number, Q is an odd number.

Look at each of these expressions and decide whether it is *always even*, *always odd* or can be *either odd or even*. Tick the correct box.

	Always even	Always odd	Either odd or even	
a $P + S$	☐	☐	☐	[1 mark]
b $P \times S$	☐	☐	☐	[1 mark]
c Q^2	☐	☐	☐	[1 mark]
d $P + Q$	☐	☐	☐	[1 mark]

This page tests you on • prime numbers • square numbers

Roots and powers

1 Here are six number cards.

a Use **three** of the cards to make this statement true.

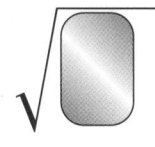  

[1 mark]

b Use **three different** cards to make this statement true.

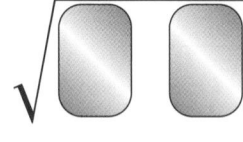  

[1 mark]

c Which is greater, $\sqrt{144}$ or 2^4?

_____ [1 mark]

d Write down the value of each number.

i $\sqrt{169}$ **ii** 5^3

_____   _____ [1 mark each]

e Write down the value of each number.

i $\sqrt[3]{64}$ **ii** 2^8

_____   _____ [1 mark each]

E

D

2 a Fill in the missing numbers.

			Units digit
4^1	=	4	4
4^2	=	16	6
4^3	=	——	——
4^4	=	——	——
4^5	=	——	——

[2 marks]

b What is the last digit of 4^{99}? Explain your answer.

_____ [1 mark]

c Which is greater, 5^6 or 6^5? Justify your answer.

_____ [1 mark]

This page tests you on   • square roots   • powers

Powers of 10

Grades

D

1 a What is the value of the digit **4** in the number 23.4?

_____ [1 mark]

b Write 10 000 in the form 10^n, where n is an integer.

_____ [1 mark]

c Write, in full, the number represented by 10^7.

_____ [1 mark]

d Fill in the missing numbers and powers.

1000		10	1	$\frac{1}{10}$		$\frac{1}{1000}$
10^3	10^2	$10^{\square}$	$10^{\square}$	10^{-1}	10^{-2}	$10^{\square}$

[1 mark]

e Write down the value of:

i 6^0 _____ [1 mark]

ii 5^1 _____ [1 mark]

D

2 a Work out:

i 3.7×10^2

_____ [1 mark]

ii 0.25×10^3

_____ [1 mark]

b Work out:

i $7.6 \div 10$

_____ [1 mark]

ii $0.65 \div 10^2$

_____ [1 mark]

c Work out:

i $30\,000 \times 400$

_____ [1 mark]

ii 600^2

_____ [1 mark]

d Work out:

i $90\,000 \div 30$

_____ [1 mark]

ii $30\,000 \div 60$

_____ [1 mark]

This page tests you on
- powers of 10
- multiplying and dividing by powers of 10
- multiplying and dividing multiples of powers of 10

Prime factors

1 a What number is represented by $2 \times 3^2 \times 5$?

_____ **[1 mark]**

b Write 70 as the product of its prime factors.

_____ **[1 mark]**

c Write 48 as the product of its prime factors.

_____ **[1 mark]**

d i Complete the prime factor tree to find the prime factors of 900.

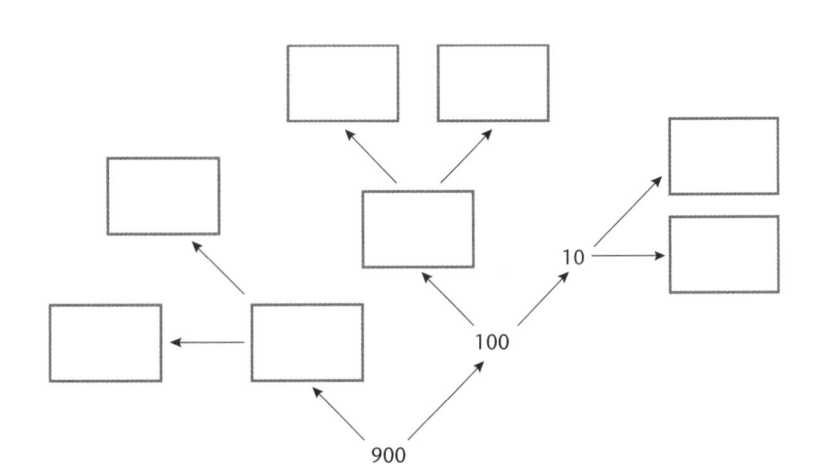

[2 marks]

ii Write 900 as the product of its prime factors, in index form.

_____ **[1 mark]**

2 a i You are given that $3x^2 = 75$.

What is the value of x?

$x =$ _____ **[1 mark]**

ii Write 150 as the product of its prime factors.

$x =$ _____ **[1 mark]**

b i You are given that $2x^3 = 54$.

What is the value of x?

$x =$ _____ **[1 mark]**

ii Write 216 as the product of its prime factors.

_____ **[1 mark]**

This page tests you on • prime factors

LCM and HCF

C

1 a Write 24 as the product of its prime factors.

_____ **[1 mark]**

b Write 60 as the product of its prime factors.

_____ **[1 mark]**

c What is the lowest common multiple of 24 and 60?

_____ **[1 mark]**

d What is the highest common factor of 24 and 60?

_____ **[1 mark]**

e In prime factor form, the number $P = 2^4 \times 3^2 \times 5$ and the number $Q = 2^2 \times 3 \times 5^2$.

   i What is the lowest common multiple of P and Q?

   Give your answer in index form.

_____ **[1 mark]**

   ii What is the highest common factor of P and Q?

   Give your answer in index form.

_____ **[1 mark]**

C

2 a You are told that p and q are prime numbers.

$p^2 q^2 = 36$

What are the values of p and q?

$p =$ _____

$q =$ _____ **[2 marks]**

b Write 360 as the product of its prime factors.

_____ **[1 mark]**

c You are told that a and b are prime numbers.

$ab^2 = 98$

What are the values of a and b?

$a =$ _____

$b =$ _____ **[2 marks]**

d Write 196 as the product of its prime factors.

_____ **[1 mark]**

This page tests you on • lowest common multiple • highest common factor

Powers

1 a Write $4^3 \times 4^5$ as a single power of 4.

_____ **[1 mark]**

b Write $6^5 \div 6^2$ as a single power of 6.

_____ **[1 mark]**

c i If $3^n = 81$, what is the value of n?

_____ **[1 mark]**

ii If $3^m = 27$, what is the value of m?

_____ **[1 mark]**

d Write down the actual value of $7^9 \div 7^7$.

_____ **[1 mark]**

e Write down the actual value of $10^4 \times 10^4$.

_____ **[1 mark]**

f Write down the actual value of $2^2 \times 5^2 \times 2^4 \times 5^4$.

_____ **[1 mark]**

C

2 a Write $x^5 \times x^2$ as a single power of x.

_____ **[1 mark]**

b Write $x^8 \div x^4$ as a single power of x.

_____ **[1 mark]**

c $2^3 \times 3^3 = 6^3$.

Which of the following expressions is the same as $a^n \times b^n$?

$(a + b)^n$ $\qquad$ ab^{2n} $\qquad$ $(ab)^n$

_____ **[1 mark]**

d $8^3 \div 2^3 = 4^3$.

Which of the following expressions is the same as $a^n \div b^n$?

$(a \div b)^n$ $\qquad$ $a \div b^n$ $\qquad$ $a^n - b^n$

_____ **[1 mark]**

C

This page tests you on • multiplying powers • dividing powers
• multiplying and dividing powers with letters

Number skills

1 a Arne uses the column method to work out 37×48. This is his working.

```
          3    7
  ×       4    8
  2      9₅    6
  1      4₂    8
  4      4     4
  1      1
```

Arne has made a mistake.

i What mistake has Arne made?

_____ **[1 mark]**

ii Work out the correct answer to 37×48.

_____ **[1 mark]**

b Berne is using the box method to work out 29×47. This is his working.

×	20	9
40	60	49
7	27	16

```
        6    0
        4    9
        2    7
  +     1    6
  1     5    2
```

Berne has made a mistake.

i What mistake has Berne made?

_____ **[1 mark]**

ii Work out the correct answer to 29×47.

_____ **[2 marks]**

2 a There are 144 plasters in a box. How many plasters will there be in 24 boxes?

_____ **[2 marks]**

b Each box of plasters costs 98p. How much will 24 boxes of plasters cost?

Give your answer in pounds and pence.

_____ **[2 marks]**

This page tests you on • long multiplication

1 a Write down the answers to these.

F

    i $1 \times 29 =$ _____

    ii $2 \times 29 =$ _____

    iii $10 \times 29 =$ _____

    iv $20 \times 29 =$ _____ **[2 marks]**

b Using the values above, or otherwise, complete this division by the chunking method.

$1508 \div 29$ 1 5 0 8

                  –   5 8 0

[2 marks]

c i Write down the answer to $1520 \div 29$.

_____ **[1 mark]**

    ii Write down the answer to $1508 \div 58$.

_____ **[1 mark]**

2 a A widget machine produces 912 widgets per hour.

F

How many widgets does it produce during a 16-hour shift?

_____ **[2 marks]**

b The widgets are packed in boxes of 24.

How many boxes will be needed to pack 912 widgets?

_____ **[2 marks]**

This page tests you on   • long division

F

1 a The school canteen has 34 tables.

Each table can seat up to 14 students.

What is the maximum number of people who could use the canteen at one time?

_____ **[2 marks]**

b The head wants to expand the canteen so it can cater for 600 students.

How many extra tables will be needed?

_____ **[2 marks]**

F

2 a This table shows the column headings for the number 23.4789.

10	1	•	$\frac{1}{10}$	$\frac{1}{100}$	$\frac{1}{1000}$	$\frac{1}{10\,000}$
2	3	•	4	7	8	9

i The number 23.4789 is multiplied by 100.

What will be the place value of the digit 4 in the **answer** to 23.4789 × 100?

_____ **[1 mark]**

ii The number 23.4789 is divided by 10.

What will be the place value of the digit 7 in the **answer** to 23.4789 ÷ 10?

_____ **[1 mark]**

b Round the number 23.4789 to:

i 1 decimal place

_____ **[1 mark]**

ii 2 decimal places

_____ **[1 mark]**

iii 3 decimal places.

_____ **[1 mark]**

This page tests you on • real-life problems • decimal places

1 a Complete the shopping bill.

3 jars of jam at £1.28 per jar	
2 kg of apples at £2.15 per kg	
5 doughnuts at 22p each	
Total	**[4 marks]**

b Work these out.

i 3 × 2.6

_____ **[1 mark]**

ii 2.4 × 2.6

_____ **[2 marks]**

c A dividend is a repayment made every few months on the amount spent.
The Co-op pays a dividend of 2.6 pence for every £1 spent.

i In three months, Derek spends £240.

How much dividend will he get?

_____ **[1 mark]**

ii Doreen received a dividend of £7.80.

How much did she spend to get this dividend?

_____ **[1 mark]**

E

2 a i Work out 6 × 2.9.

_____ **[1 mark]**

ii Work out 4.6 × 2.9.

_____ **[2 marks]**

b What is the cost of 2.9 kg of coffee beans at £4.60 per kilogram?

_____ **[1 mark]**

F

This page tests you on
- adding and subtracting decimals
- multiplying and dividing decimals by single-digit numbers
- long multiplication with decimals
- multiplying decimals

More fractions

D-C

1 a Work out $\frac{3}{4} + \frac{2}{5}$.

Give your answer as a mixed number.

_____ **[2 marks]**

b Work out $3\frac{2}{3} - 1\frac{4}{5}$.

Give your answer as a mixed number.

_____ **[2 marks]**

c On an aeroplane, two-fifths of the passengers were British, one-quarter were German, one-sixth were American and the rest were French.

What fraction of the passengers are French?

_____ **[2 marks]**

D-C

2 a Work out $2\frac{1}{2} \times 1\frac{2}{5}$.

_____ **[2 marks]**

b Work out $3\frac{3}{10} \div 2\frac{2}{5}$.

Give your answer as a mixed number.

_____ **[2 marks]**

c Work out the area of this triangle.

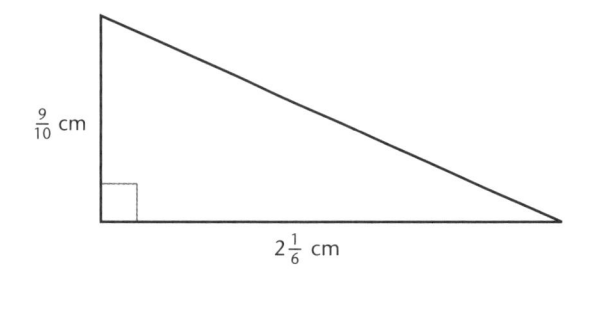

$\frac{9}{10}$ cm

$2\frac{1}{6}$ cm

_____ cm² **[2 marks]**

This page tests you on
- adding and subtracting fractions
- multiplying fractions • dividing fractions

More number

1 a Complete the following calculations.

i

 ×  = ⬜ **[1 mark]**

ii

 × ⬜ = **12** **[1 mark]**

iii

⬜ ÷ **-5** = **+4** **[1 mark]**

b Complete this sentence, using **two negative** numbers.

⬜ − ⬜ = **+2** **[1 mark]**

c Look at these numbers.

−4, −3, −2, 0, 2, 5, 9

i Mazy is asked to pick out the square numbers. She chooses −4 and 9.

Explain why Mazy is wrong.

_____ **[1 mark]**

ii Work out the mean of the numbers.

_____

_____ **[2 marks]**

D-C

2 a Round each of these numbers to one significant figure.

i 52.1 **ii** 0.38

_____ _____ **[1 mark each]**

b Find an approximate value for $\dfrac{52.1 \times 39.6}{18.7 - 11.1}$.

_____ **[1 mark]**

c Find an approximate value for $\dfrac{52.1 - 29.7}{0.38}$.

_____ **[2 marks]**

C

This page tests you on
- multiplying and dividing with negative numbers
- rounding to one significant figure
- approximation of calculations

Ratio

1 The angles of a quadrilateral are in the ratio $2:3:5:8$.

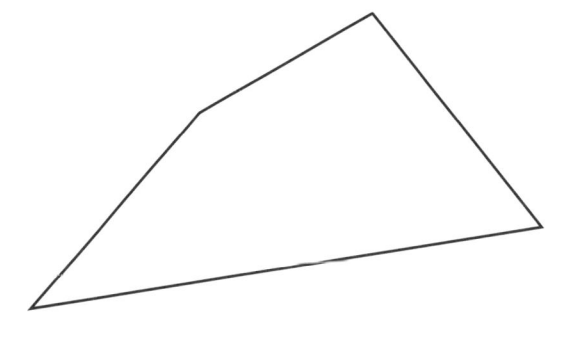

What is the value of the largest angle?

_____ ° **[3 marks]**

2 a Write the ratio $12:9$ in its simplest form.

_____ **[1 mark]**

b Write the ratio $5:2$ in the form $1:n$.

_____ **[1 mark]**

c A fruit drink is made from orange juice and cranberry juice in the ratio $5:3$.

If 1 litre of the drink is made, how much of the drink is cranberry juice?

_____ **[2 marks]**

3 In a tutor group the ratio of boys to girls is $3:4$.

There are 15 boys in the form.

How many students are there in the form altogether?

_____ **[2 marks]**

This page tests you on • ratio • dividing amounts in ratios
• calculating with ratios

Speed and proportion

1 A ferry covers the 72 kilometres between Holyhead and Dublin in $2\frac{1}{4}$ hours.

   a What is the average speed of the ferry?

    State the units of your answer.

   _____ **[3 marks]**

   b For the first 15 minutes and the last 15 minutes, the Ferry is manoeuvring in and out of the ports. During this time the average speed is 18 km per hour.

    What is the average speed of the ferry during the rest of the journey?

   _____ **[2 marks]**

2 A car uses 50 litres of petrol in driving 275 miles.

   a How much petrol will the car use in driving 165 miles?

   _____ **[2 marks]**

   b How many miles can the car drive on 26 litres of petrol?

   _____ **[1 mark]**

3 Nutty Flake cereal is sold in two sizes.

   The handy size contains 600 g and costs £1.55.

   The large size contains 800 g and costs £2.20.

   Which size is the better value?

   _____ **[2 marks]**

This page tests you on
- speed, time and distance
- direct proportion problems • best buys

Percentages

C

1 a Complete this table of equivalent fractions, decimals and percentages.

Decimal	Fraction	Percentage
0.35		
	$\frac{4}{5}$	
		90%

[3 marks]

b i What fraction of this diagram is shaded?

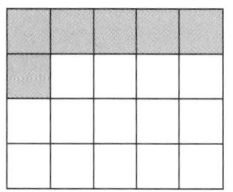

Give your answer in its simplest form.

_____ [1 mark]

ii What percentage is **not** shaded?

_____ [1 mark]

c Write these values in order of size, smallest first.

0.6 $\frac{11}{20}$ 57% $\frac{14}{25}$

_____ [2 marks]

D

2 a A car cost £6000 new.

It depreciated in value by 12% in the first year.

It then depreciated in value by 10% in the second year.

Which of these calculations shows the value of the car after two years?

Circle the correct answer.

6000×0.78 $6000 \times 0.88 \times 0.9$ $6000 \times 88 \times 90$ $6000 - 2200$ [1 mark]

b VAT is charged at $17\frac{1}{2}$%.

A quick way to work out the VAT on an item is to work out 10%, then divide this by 2 to get 5%, then divide this by 2 to get $2\frac{1}{2}$%. Add these values all together.

Use this method to work out the VAT on an item costing £68.

_____ [2 marks]

This page tests you on
- equivalent percentages, fractions and decimals
- the percentage multiplier

1 A washing machine normally costs £350.

Its price is reduced by 15% in a sale.

a What is 15% of £350?

£_____ **[2 marks]**

b What is the sale price of the washing machine?

£_____ **[1 mark]**

E

2 a A computer costs £700, not including VAT.

VAT is charged at $17\frac{1}{2}$%.

What is the cost of the computer when VAT is added?

£_____ **[2 marks]**

b The price of a printer is reduced by 12% in a sale.

The original price of the printer was £250.

What is the price of the printer in the sale?

£_____ **[2 marks]**

D

3 In the first week it was operational, a new bus route carried a total of 2250 people.

In the second week it carried 2655 people.

What is the percentage increase in the number of passengers from the first week to the second?

_____ **[2 marks]**

C

This page tests you on
- calculating a percentage of a quantity
- percentage increase or decrease
- one quantity as a percentage of another

Number checklist

I can...

- [ ] recall the times tables up to 10×10
- [ ] use BODMAS to do calculations in the correct order
- [ ] identify the place value of digits in whole numbers
- [ ] round numbers to the nearest 10 or 100
- [ ] add and subtract numbers with up to four digits without a calculator
- [ ] multiply numbers by a single-digit number
- [ ] state what fraction of a shape is shaded
- [ ] shade in a fraction of a shape
- [ ] add and subtract simple fractions with the same denominator
- [ ] recognise equivalent fractions
- [ ] cancel a fraction
- [ ] change top-heavy fractions into mixed numbers and vice versa
- [ ] find a fraction of an integer
- [ ] recognise the multiples of the first 10 whole numbers
- [ ] recognise square numbers up to 100
- [ ] find equivalent fractions, decimals and percentages
- [ ] know that a number on the left on a number line is smaller than a number on the right
- [ ] read negative numbers on scales such as thermometers

You are working at (Grade G) level.

- [ ] divide numbers by a single-digit number
- [ ] put fractions in order of size
- [ ] add fractions with different denominators
- [ ] solve fraction problems expressed in words
- [ ] compare fractions of quantities
- [ ] find factors of numbers less than 100
- [ ] add and subtract with negative numbers
- [ ] write down the squares of numbers up to 15×15
- [ ] write down the cubes of 1, 2, 3, 4, 5 and 10
- [ ] use a calculator to find square roots
- [ ] do long multiplication
- [ ] do long division
- [ ] solve real-life problems involving multiplication and division
- [ ] round decimal numbers to one, two or three decimal places
- [ ] find percentages of a quantity
- [ ] change mixed numbers into top-heavy fractions

You are working at (Grade F) level.

- [ ] multiply fractions
- [ ] add and subtract mixed numbers
- [ ] calculate powers of numbers
- [ ] recognise prime numbers under 100
- [ ] use the four rules with decimals
- [ ] change decimals to fractions
- [ ] change fractions to decimals
- [ ] simplify a ratio
- [ ] find a percentage of any quantity

You are working at (Grade E) level.

- [ ] work out one quantity as a fraction of another
- [ ] solve problems using negative numbers
- [ ] multiply and divide by powers of 10
- [ ] multiply together numbers that are multiples of powers of 10
- [ ] round numbers to one significant figure
- [ ] estimate the answer to a calculation
- [ ] order lists of numbers containing decimals, fractions and percentages
- [ ] multiply and divide fractions
- [ ] calculate with speed, distance and time
- [ ] compare prices to find 'best buys'
- [ ] find the new value after a percentage increase or decrease
- [ ] find one quantity as a percentage of another
- [ ] solve problems involving simple negative numbers
- [ ] multiply and divide fractions

You are working at (Grade D) level.

- [ ] work out a reciprocal
- [ ] recognise and work out terminating and recurring decimals
- [ ] write a number as a product of prime factors
- [ ] use the index laws to simplify calculations and expressions
- [ ] multiply and divide with negative numbers
- [ ] multiply and divide with mixed numbers
- [ ] find a percentage increase
- [ ] work out the LCM and HCF of two numbers
- [ ] solve problems using ratio in appropriate situations

You are working at (Grade C) level.

Perimeter and area

1 Here is a rectangle.

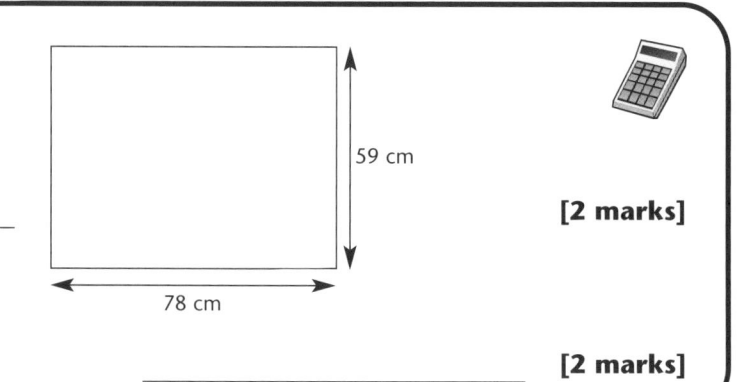

a Find the perimeter of the rectangle.

State the units of your answer.

_____

59 cm

[2 marks]

b Find the area of the rectangle.

State the units of your answer.

78 cm

[2 marks]

2 a The map of an island is drawn on the centimeter-square grid.

The scale is 1 cm represents 1 km.

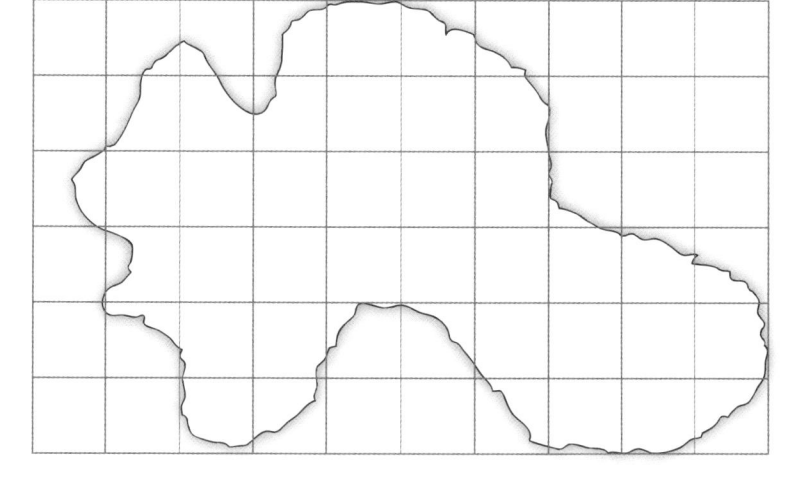

Estimate the area of the island.

State the units of your answer.

_____ **[2 marks]**

b The diagram shows a trapezium drawn on a centimetre-square grid.

By counting squares, or otherwise, find the area of the trapezium.

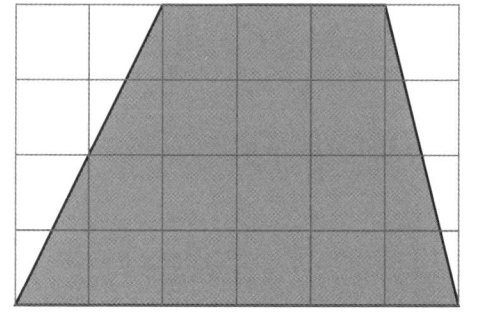

cm² **[2 marks]**

This page tests you on
- perimeter
- area of irregular shapes (counting squares)
- area of a rectangle

Grades

1 Calculate the area of this shape. D

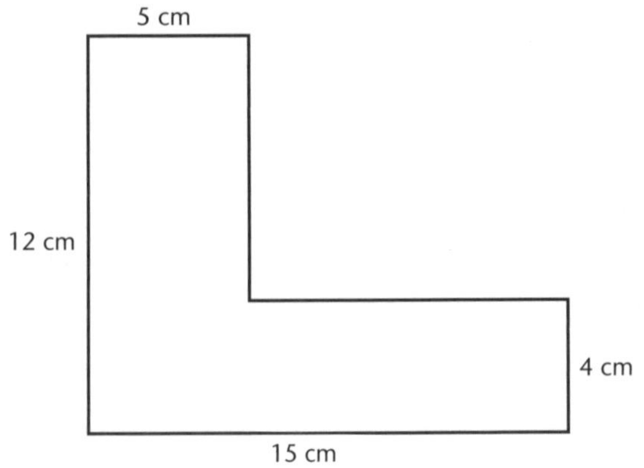
5 cm
12 cm
4 cm
15 cm

______ cm^2 **[2 marks]**

2 a Calculate the area of this triangle. D

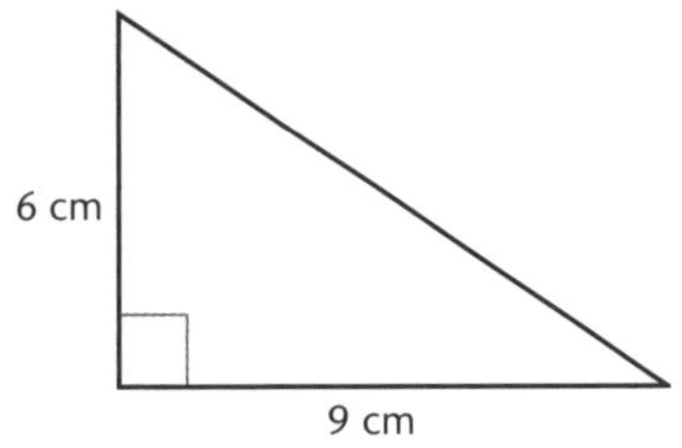
6 cm
9 cm

______ cm^2 **[2 marks]**

b Calculate the area of this shape.

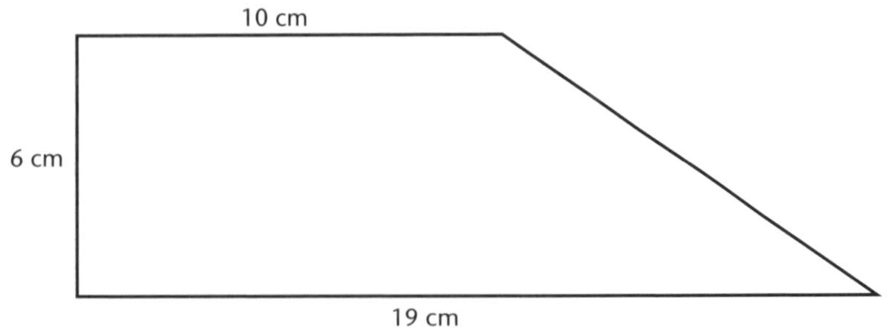
10 cm
6 cm
19 cm

______ cm^2 **[2 marks]**

This page tests you on • area of a compound shape • area of a triangle

1 a The parallelogram is drawn on a centimetre-square grid.

Find the area of the parallelogram.

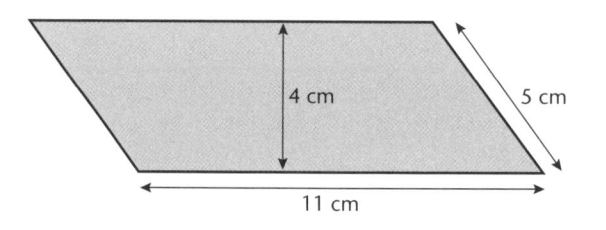

_____ cm² **[2 marks]**

b Calculate the area of this parallelogram.

4 cm

5 cm

11 cm

_____ cm² **[2 marks]**

D

2 Calculate the area of this trapezium.

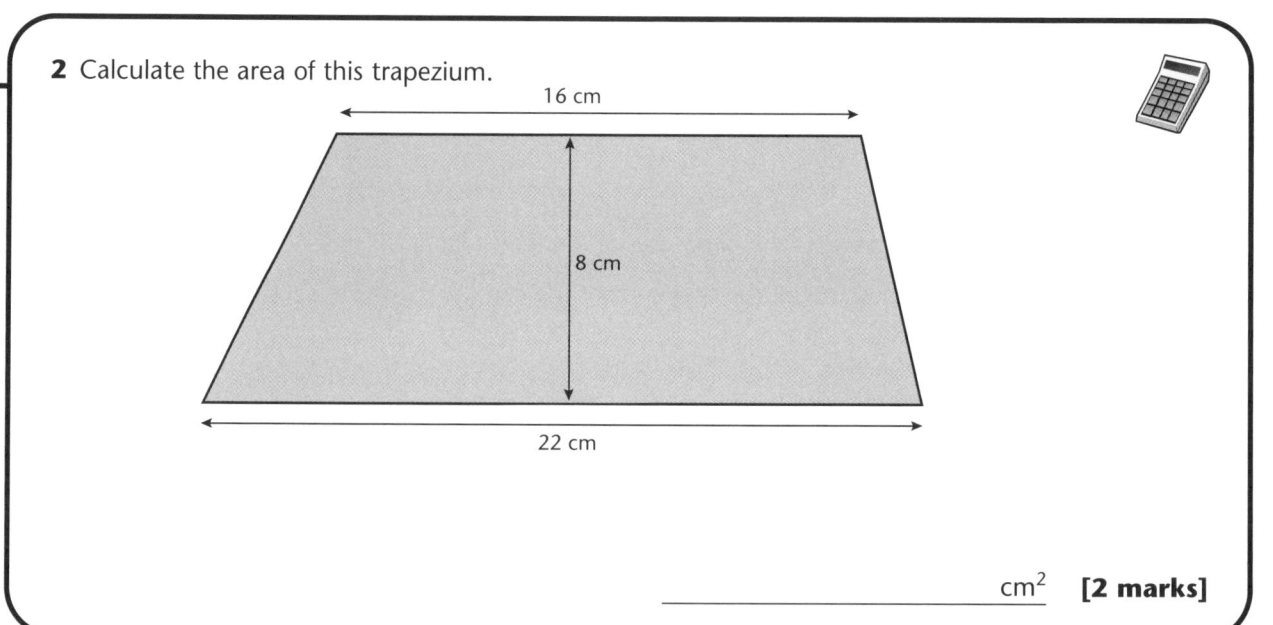

16 cm

8 cm

22 cm

_____ cm² **[2 marks]**

This page tests you on   • area of a parallelogram   • area of a trapezium

Dimensional analysis

1 A cuboid has sides of length x, y and z cm.

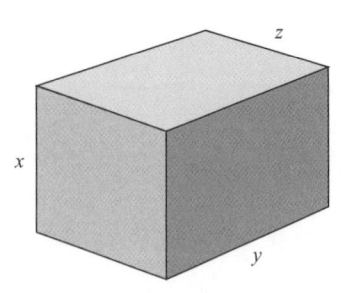

One of the following formulae represents the total lengths of the edges (L).

One of them represents the total area of the faces (A).

One of them represents the total volume (V).

Indicate which is which.

- $2xz + 2yz + 2xy$ represents the total _____ **[1 mark]**
- xyz represents the total _____ **[1 mark]**
- $4x + 4y + 4z$ represents the total _____ **[1 mark]**

2 A can of beans is a cylinder with a radius r cm and height h cm.

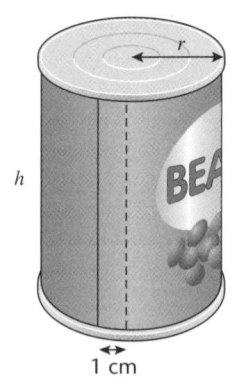

The can has a label around it that is glued together with an overlap of 1 centimetre.

One of these formulae represents the perimeter of the label (P).

One of them represents the area of the two ends of the can (A).

One of them represents the volume of the can (V).

Indicate which is which.

- $2\pi r^2$ represents the _____ **[1 mark]**
- $4\pi r + 2h + 2$ represents the _____ **[1 mark]**
- $\pi r^2 h$ represents the _____ **[1 mark]**

This page tests you on • dimensional analysis • dimensions of length • dimensions of area • dimensions of volume

Symmetry

G

1

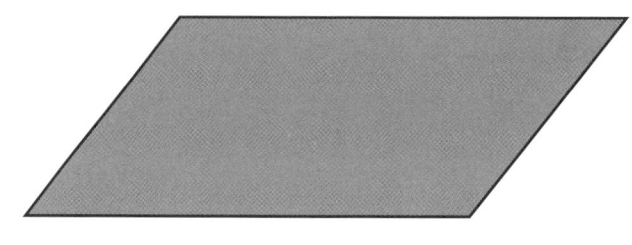

a Which of the letters above have line symmetry?

_____ **[2 marks]**

b Which of the letters above have rotational symmetry of order 2?

_____ **[1 mark]**

c

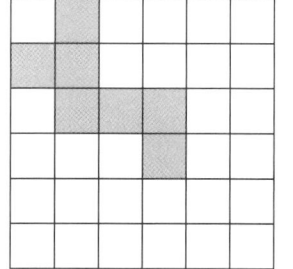

i How many lines of symmetry does the parallelogram have?

_____ **[1 mark]**

ii What is the order of rotational symmetry of a parallelogram?

_____ **[1 mark]**

F

2 a Shade in **five** more squares so that the pattern has no lines of symmetry and rotational symmetry of order 2.

[1 mark]

b The diagram shows an octahedron made of two equal square-based pyramids joined by their bases.

How many planes of symmetry does this octahedron have?

_____ **[1 mark]**

This page tests you on • lines of symmetry • rotational symmetry
• planes of symmetry

Angles

1 a Measure the following angles.

i

ii

_____ °

_____ ° **[2 marks]**

b Draw an angle of 55°.

[1 mark]

2 a The diagram shows three angles on a straight line.

Work out the value of x.

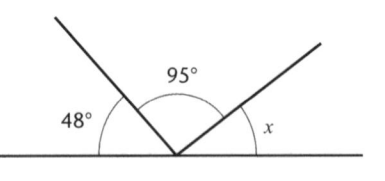

_____ ° **[1 mark]**

b The diagram shows three angles meeting at a point.

Work out the value of x.

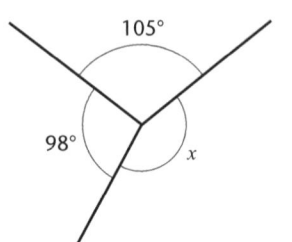

_____ ° **[1 mark]**

This page tests you on • measuring and drawing angles • angle facts

E

1 a This triangle has two equal sides.

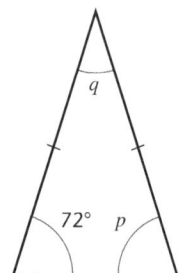

i What name is given to this type of triangle?

_____ **[1 mark]**

ii Find the values of p and q.

$p =$ _____ °

$q =$ _____ ° **[2 marks]**

b Work out the size of the angle marked x.

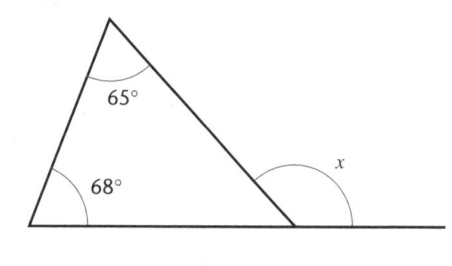

_____ ° **[2 marks]**

E

2 The diagram shows a kite.

Work out the size of the angle marked y.

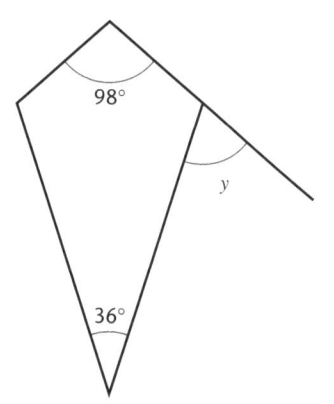

_____ ° **[2 marks]**

Polygons

1 a The diagram shows a regular octagon.

O is the centre of the octagon.

Calculate the sizes of angles p, q and r.

$p =$ _____ °

$q =$ _____ °

$r =$ _____ ° **[3 marks]**

b Explain why the interior angles of a pentagon add up to 540°.

_____

_____

_____ **[2 marks]**

2 a The diagram shows three sides of a regular polygon.

The exterior angle is 36°.

How many sides does the polygon have altogether?

_____ **[2 marks]**

b The interior angle of a regular polygon is 160°.

Explain why the polygon must have 18 sides.

_____

_____

_____ **[2 marks]**

This page tests you on • polygons • regular polygons
• interior and exterior angles in a regular polygon

Parallel lines and angles

C

1 In the diagram, QR is parallel to LM.

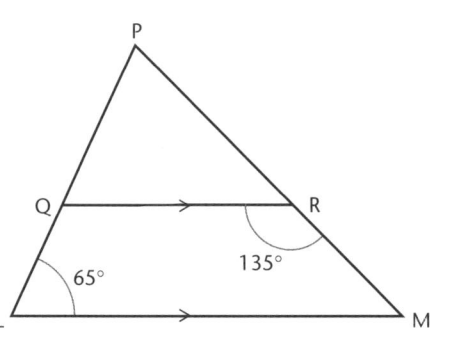

a Write down the size of angle RML.

Give a reason for your answer.

∠RML = _____ ° **[1 mark]**

Reason: _____ **[1 mark]**

b Write down the size of angle PQR.

Give a reason for your answer.

∠PQR = _____ ° **[1 mark]**

Reason: _____ **[1 mark]**

c Work out the size of angle QPR.

∠QPR = _____ ° **[1 mark]**

C

2 The lines AB and CD are parallel.

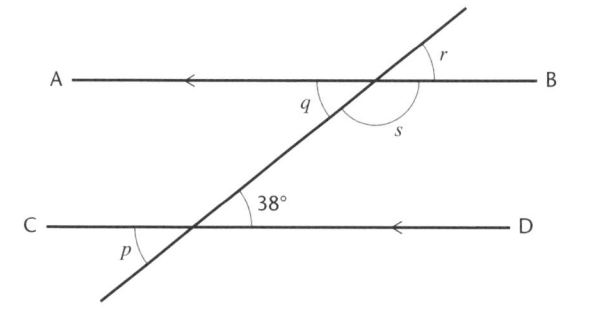

Write down the sizes of angles p, q, r and s, in each case give the reason in relation to the given angle of 38°.

p = _____° because it is _____ to the given angle of 38°. **[2 marks]**

q = _____° because it is _____ to the given angle of 38°. **[2 marks]**

r = _____° because it is _____ to the given angle of 38°. **[2 marks]**

s = _____° because it is _____ to the given angle of 38°. **[2 marks]**

This page tests you on • two parallel lines and a transversal • alternate angles
• corresponding angles • opposite angles
• interior angles

Quadrilaterals

D

1 a Jonathan is describing a quadrilateral.

What quadrilateral is he describing?

It has no lines
of symmetry and has
rotational symmetry
of order 2.

The diagonals
cross at right angles
and all the sides
are equal.

_____ **[1 mark]**

b Marie is describing another quadrilateral.

i Write down the name of a quadrilateral
that Marie could be describing.

_____ **[1 mark]**

ii Write down the name of a different
quadrilateral that Marie could be
describing.

_____ **[1 mark]**

C

2 The diagram shows a kite, ABCD, attached
to a parallelogram, CDEF.

Angle BAD = 100°, angle CFE = 60°.

When the side of the kite is extended
it passes along the diagonal of the
parallelogram.

Use the properties of quadrilaterals
to work out the size of angle CED.

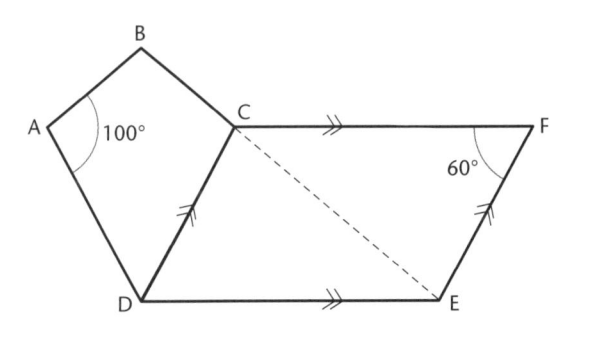

∠CED = _____ ° **[4 marks]**

This page tests you on • special quadrilaterals

Bearings

D

1 This map shows the positions of four towns, Althorp, Beeton, Cowton and Deepdale. The scale is 1 cm to 1 kilometre.

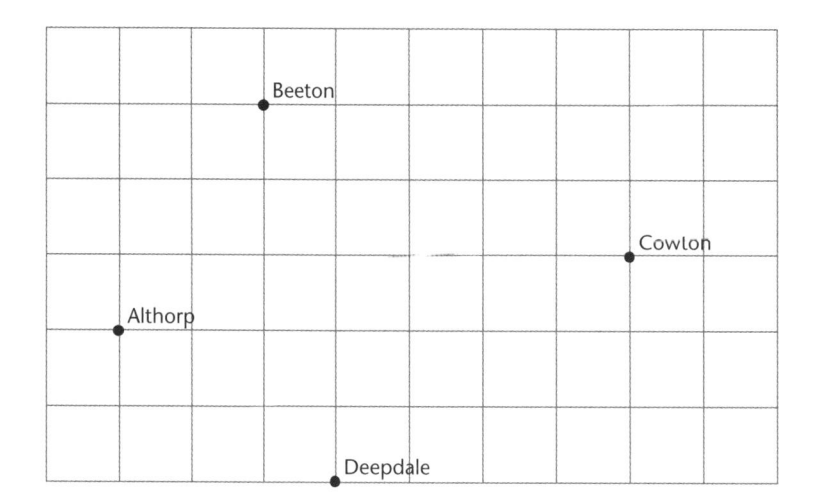

Using a ruler and protractor, find the distance and bearing of:

a Beeton from Althorp _____ km at _____ ° **[2 marks]**

b Deepdale from Beeton _____ km at _____ ° **[2 marks]**

c Deepdale from Cowton _____ km at _____ ° **[2 marks]**

d Althorp from Deepdale _____ km at _____ ° **[2 marks]**

C

2 Brian walks in a perfect square.

He starts by walking north for 100 m and then turning right.

He then continues walking for 100 m then turning right, doing it twice more until he is back to his starting point.

Write down the four bearings of the directions in which he walks.

_____ **[4 marks]**

Circles

1 From this list of words, fill in the missing words that describe parts of the circle on the diagram.

Chord   Tangent   Radius   Diameter

O is the centre of the circle.

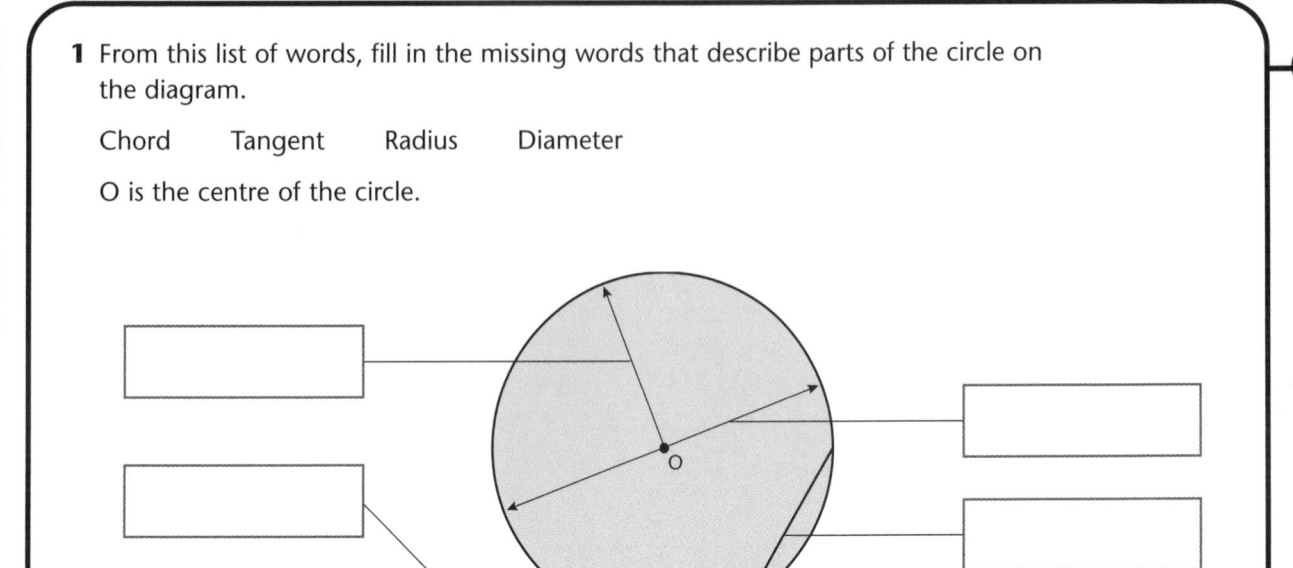

[4 marks]

F

2 a Work out the area of a circle of radius 12 cm.

Give your answer to 1 decimal place.

_____ cm^2 **[2 marks]**

b Work out the circumference of a circle of diameter 20 cm.

Give your answer to 1 decimal place.

_____ cm   **[2 marks]**

D

3 Work out the area of a semicircle of diameter 20 cm.

Give your answer in terms of π.

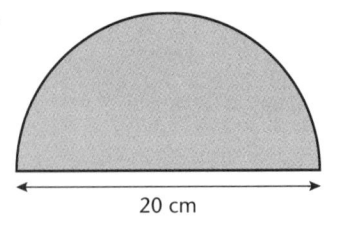

20 cm

_____ cm^2 **[2 marks]**

C

This page tests you on   • circles   • circumference of a circle   • area of a circle

Scales

1 a The thermometer shows the temperature outside Frank's local garage on a hot summer day. What temperature does the thermometer show?

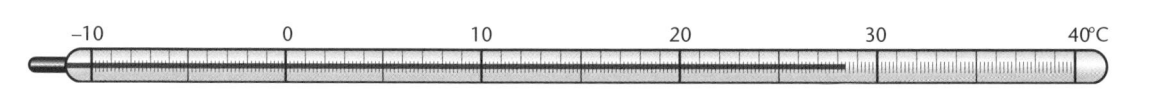

_____ °C   **[1 mark]**

b Later, when Frank was driving home, the speedometer looked like this.

What speed was Frank doing?

State the units of your answer.

_____ **[2 marks]**

c At the same time the car rev counter showed 3300 rpm.

Draw an arrow to show 3300 rpm on the scale.

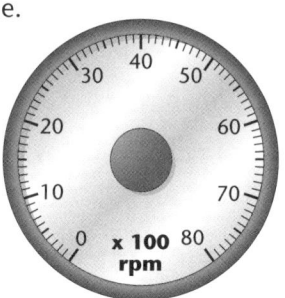

[1 mark]

2 The picture shows a coastguard with a beached whale.

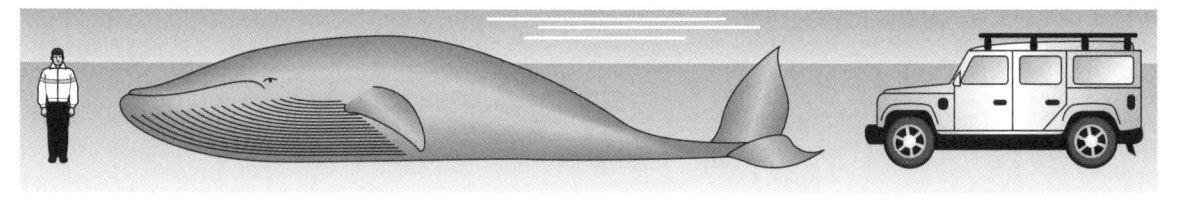

Estimate the length of the whale.

Give your answer in metres.

_____ m   **[2 marks]**

This page tests you on   • scales • sensible estimates

Scales and drawing

F

1 The diagram shows a line AB and a point C, drawn on a centimetre-square grid.

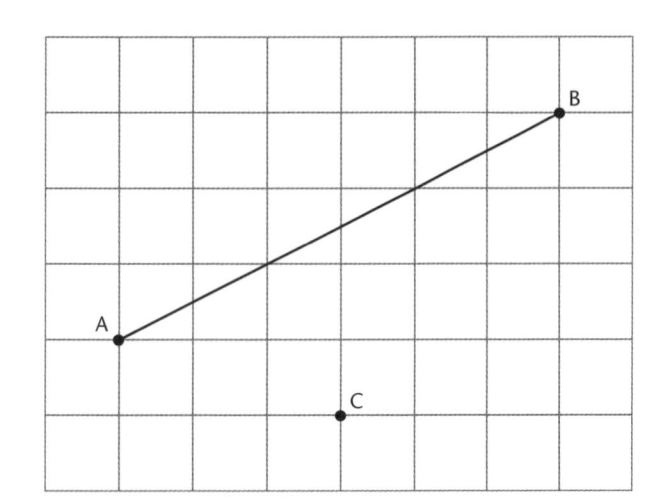

a Measure the length of the line AB, in centimetres. _____ cm   **[1 mark]**

b Mark the midpoint of AB with a cross.   **[1 mark]**

c Draw a line through the point C, perpendicular to the line AB.   **[1 mark]**

d The diagram represents a map with a scale of 1 cm to 5 km.   **[1 mark]**

  Work out the real distance represented by BC.

_____ km   **[2 marks]**

2 The net of a solid is shown, drawn to scale.

F

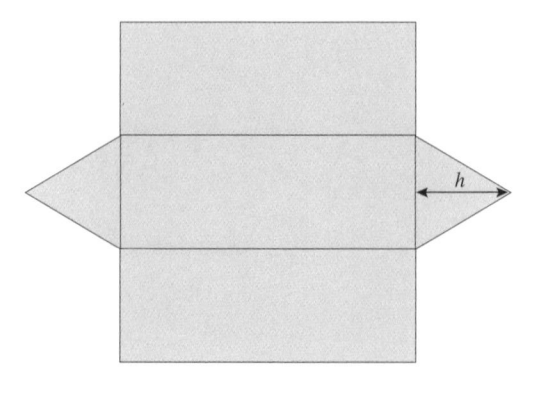

a What is the name of the solid for which this is the net?

_____   **[1 mark]**

b Measure the height of the triangle, h, shown on the net.

_____ cm   **[1 mark]**

c By taking appropriate measurements, work out the surface area of the net.

_____ cm^2 **[3 marks]**

This page tests you on   • scale drawing   • nets

3-D drawing

F

1 The diagram shows a prism, with a T-shaped cross-section, drawn on a one-centimetre isometric grid.

a What is the volume of the prism? _____ cm³ **[1 mark]**

b Draw the side elevation of the prism, from A.

[1 mark]

F

2 The diagram shows the plan and both side elevations of a solid made from five one-centimetre cubes.

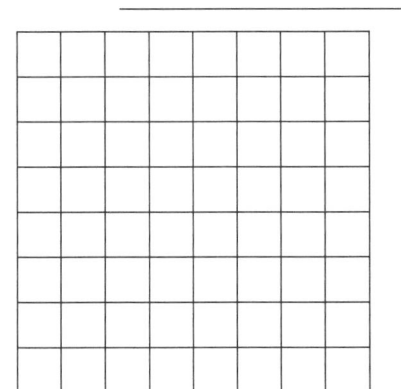

Plan   Front elevation   Side elevation

Draw an isometric view of the solid on the grid below.

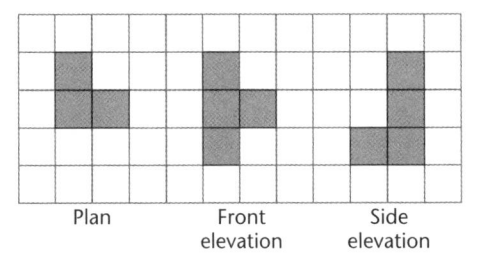

[2 marks]

Congruency and tessellations

1 The grid shows six shapes A, B, C, D, E and F.

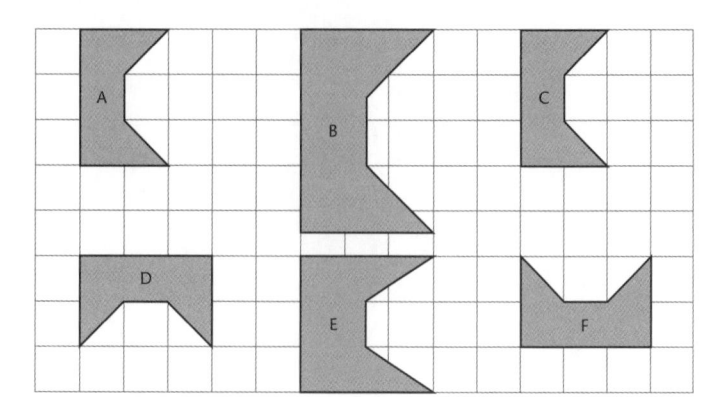

a Write down the letters of the shapes that are congruent to shape A.

_____ **[1 mark]**

b Which shape is similar to shape A?

_____ **[1 mark]**

2 a The diagram shows a tessellation of an isosceles triangle.

Explain what is meant by a *tessellation*.

_____

_____ **[1 mark]**

b Use the shape shown to draw a tessellation.

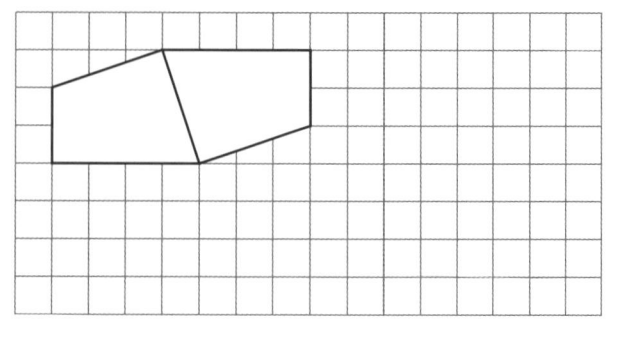

Draw at least six more shapes to show the tessellation clearly. **[1 mark]**

This page tests you on • congruent shapes • tessellations

Transformations

Grades

C

1 a Describe the transformation that takes the shaded triangle to triangle A.

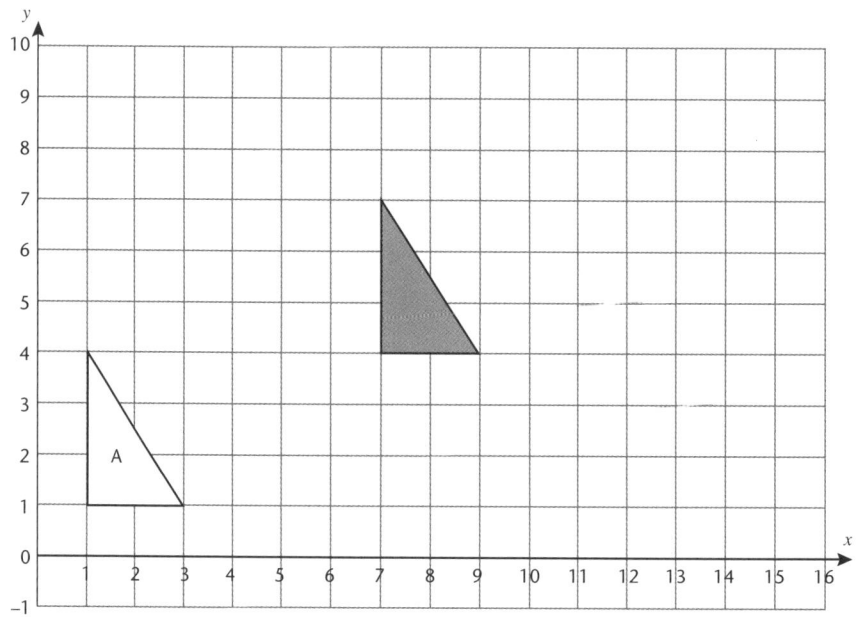

_____

_____ **[2 marks]**

b Translate the shaded triangle by $\binom{-4}{2}$. Label the image B. **[1 mark]**

c The shaded triangle is translated by $\binom{7}{-5}$ to give triangle C.

What **vector** will translate triangle C to the shaded triangle?

_____ **[1 mark]**

D

2

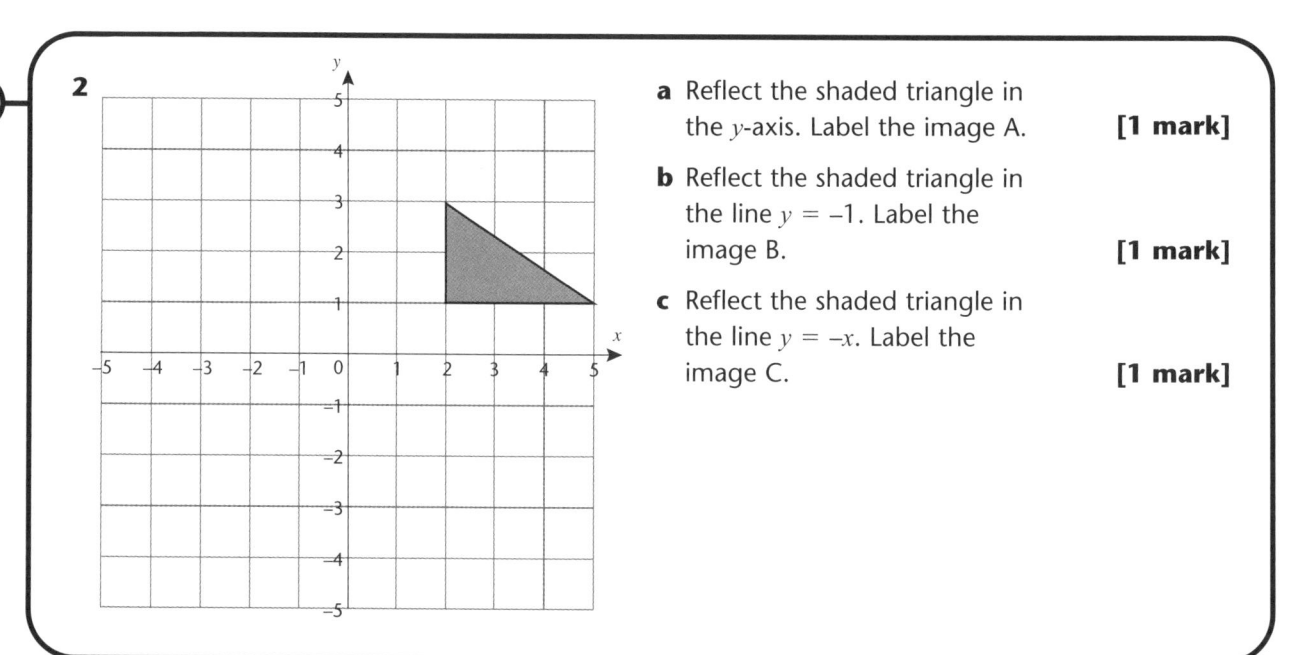

a Reflect the shaded triangle in the y-axis. Label the image A. **[1 mark]**

b Reflect the shaded triangle in the line $y = -1$. Label the image B. **[1 mark]**

c Reflect the shaded triangle in the line $y = -x$. Label the image C. **[1 mark]**

This page tests you on • transformations • translations • reflections

1

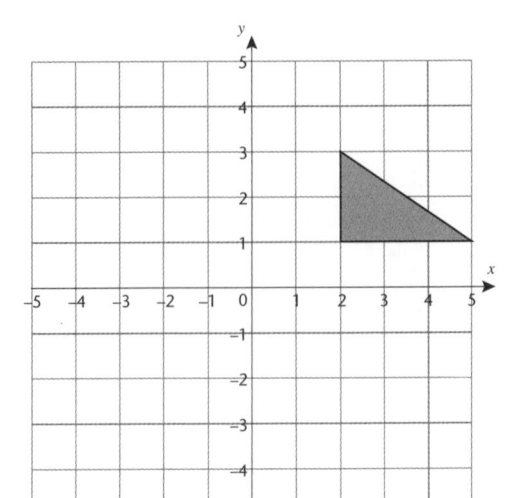

D

a Rotate the shaded triangle by 90° clockwise about (1, 0). Label the image A. **[1 mark]**

b Rotate the shaded triangle by a half-turn about (1, 3). Label the image B. **[1 mark]**

c What rotation will take triangle A to triangle B?

_____ **[3 marks]**

2

D

a What transformation takes the shaded triangle to triangle A?

_____ **[2 marks]**

b Draw the image after the shaded triangle is enlarged by a scale factor $\frac{1}{4}$ centred on (1, 0). **[1 mark]**

This page tests you on • rotations • enlargements

Constructions

1 Make an accurate drawing of this triangle.

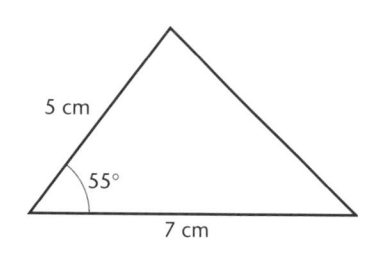

5 cm

55°

7 cm

[3 marks]

2 a Using compasses and a ruler, construct an angle of 60° at the point A.

A •————————————

b i Use compasses and a ruler to construct this triangle accurately.

[2 marks]

B

6 cm

60°

A

8 cm

C

[3 marks]

ii Measure the length of the line BC. _____ cm **[1 mark]**

This page tests you on • constructing triangles • constructing an angle of 60°

1 Use compasses and a ruler to do these constructions.

  a Construct the perpendicular bisector of AB.

A ●

● B

[2 marks]

  b Construct the perpendicular at the point C to the line L.

——————————————————●———————————— L
                   C

[2 marks]

C

2 Use compasses and ruler to do these constructions.

  a Construct the perpendicular bisector of the line L.

——————————————— L

[2 marks]

  b Construct the bisector of angle ABC.

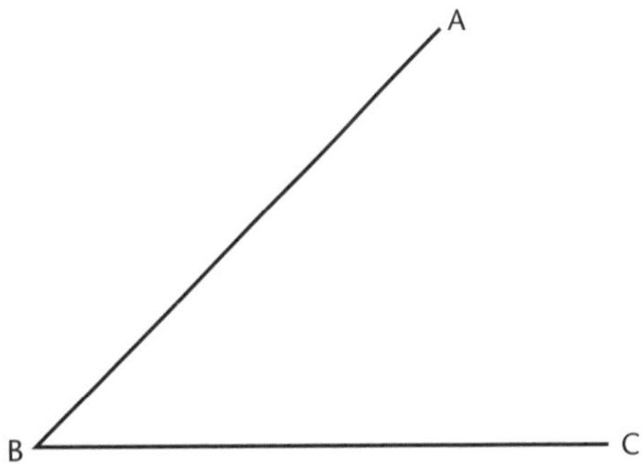

A

B ——————————————— C

[2 marks]

C

This page tests you on   • the perpendicular bisector   • the angle bisector
                            • the perpendicular at a point on a line

Constructions and loci

C

1 Use compasses and a ruler to construct the perpendicular from the point C to the line L.

• C

L

[2 marks]

C

2 The diagram, which is drawn to scale, shows a flat, rectangular lawn of length 10 m and width 6 m, with a circular flower bed of radius 2 m.

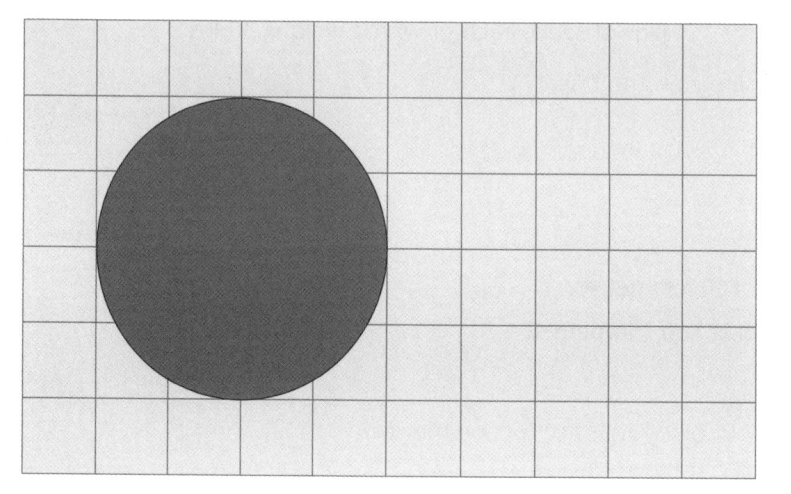

Scale: 1 cm represents 1 m.

A tree is going to be planted in the garden.

It has to be at least 1 metre from the edge of the garden and at least 2 metres from the flower bed.

a Draw a circle to show the area around the flower bed where the tree *cannot* be planted.

[1 mark]

b Show the area of the garden in which the tree *can* be planted.

[1 mark]

This page tests you on
- the perpendicular from a point to a line
- loci • practical problems

Units

1 An old water butt is labelled: 'When full contains 50 gallons'.

Mary has a watering can that holds 9 litres.

a How many centilitres is 9 litres?

_____ cl **[1 mark]**

b Approximately how many times can Mary fill the watering can from the water butt when it is full?

_____ **[2 marks]**

c A bottle of weedkiller says: 'Mix 200 g with 10 litres of water.'

How many grams of weedkiller will Mary have to mix with 9 litres of water?

_____ g **[2 marks]**

2 a The safety instructions for Ahmed's trailer say:

'Load not to exceed 150 kg.'

Ahmed wants to carry 12 bags of sand, each of which weighs 30 lbs.

Can he carry them safely on the trailer?

_____ **[1 mark]**

b Ahmed has to drive 160 kilometres.

i How many metres is 160 kilometres?

_____ m **[1 mark]**

ii Approximately how many miles is 160 kilometres?

_____ miles **[1 mark]**

c Ahmed's car travels 30 miles to the gallon.

His tank contains 20 litres.

Will he have enough fuel in the tank to drive 160 kilometres?

_____ **[2 marks]**

This page tests you on • systems of measurement • the metric system • the imperial system • conversion factors

Surface area and volume of 3-D shapes

F

1 A rectangle measures 20 centimetres by 30 centimetres.

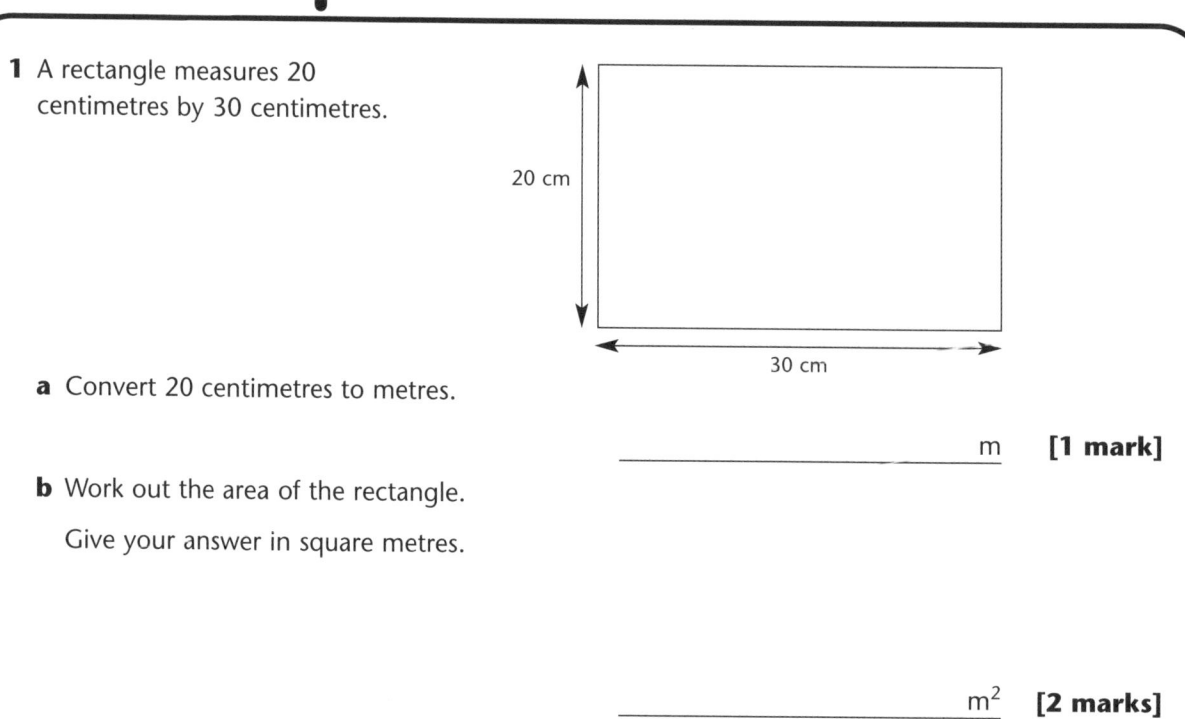

20 cm

30 cm

a Convert 20 centimetres to metres.

_____ m **[1 mark]**

b Work out the area of the rectangle.

Give your answer in square metres.

_____ m² **[2 marks]**

D

2 The diagram shows a cuboid, drawn on a centimetre isometric grid.

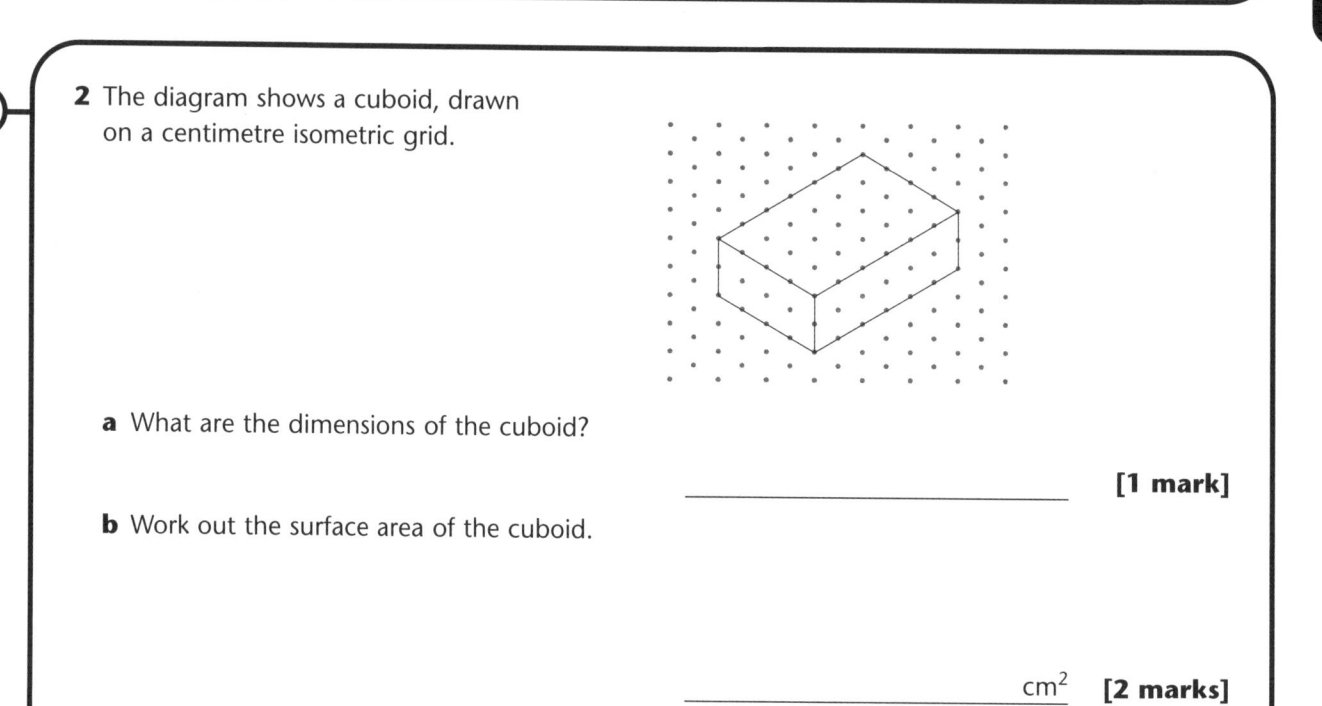

a What are the dimensions of the cuboid?

_____ **[1 mark]**

b Work out the surface area of the cuboid.

_____ cm² **[2 marks]**

c What is the volume of the cuboid?

State the units of your answer.

_____ **[2 marks]**

This page tests you on • units of length, area and volume
• surface area of a cuboid • volume of a cuboid

Density and prisms

1 A block of metal has a volume of 750 cm³.

It has a mass of 5.1 kg.

Calculate the density of the metal.

State the units of your answer.

_____ **[2 marks]**

C

2 A triangular prism has dimensions as shown.

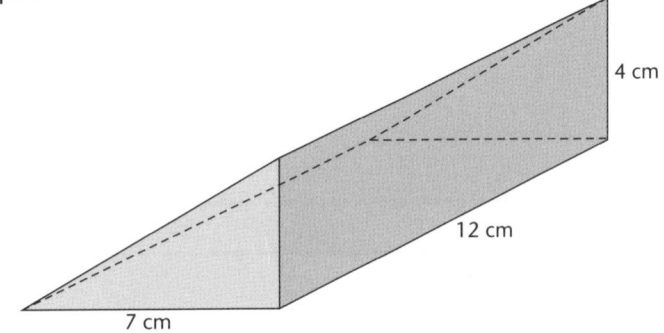

4 cm

12 cm

7 cm

a Calculate the cross-sectional area of the prism.

_____ cm² **[1 mark]**

b Calculate the volume of the prism.

_____ cm³ **[2 marks]**

D

3 A cylinder has a radius of 4 cm and a height of 10 cm.

What is the volume of the cylinder?

Give your answer in terms of π.

_____ cm³ **[2 marks]**

C

This page tests you on • density • prisms and cylinders

Pythagoras' theorem

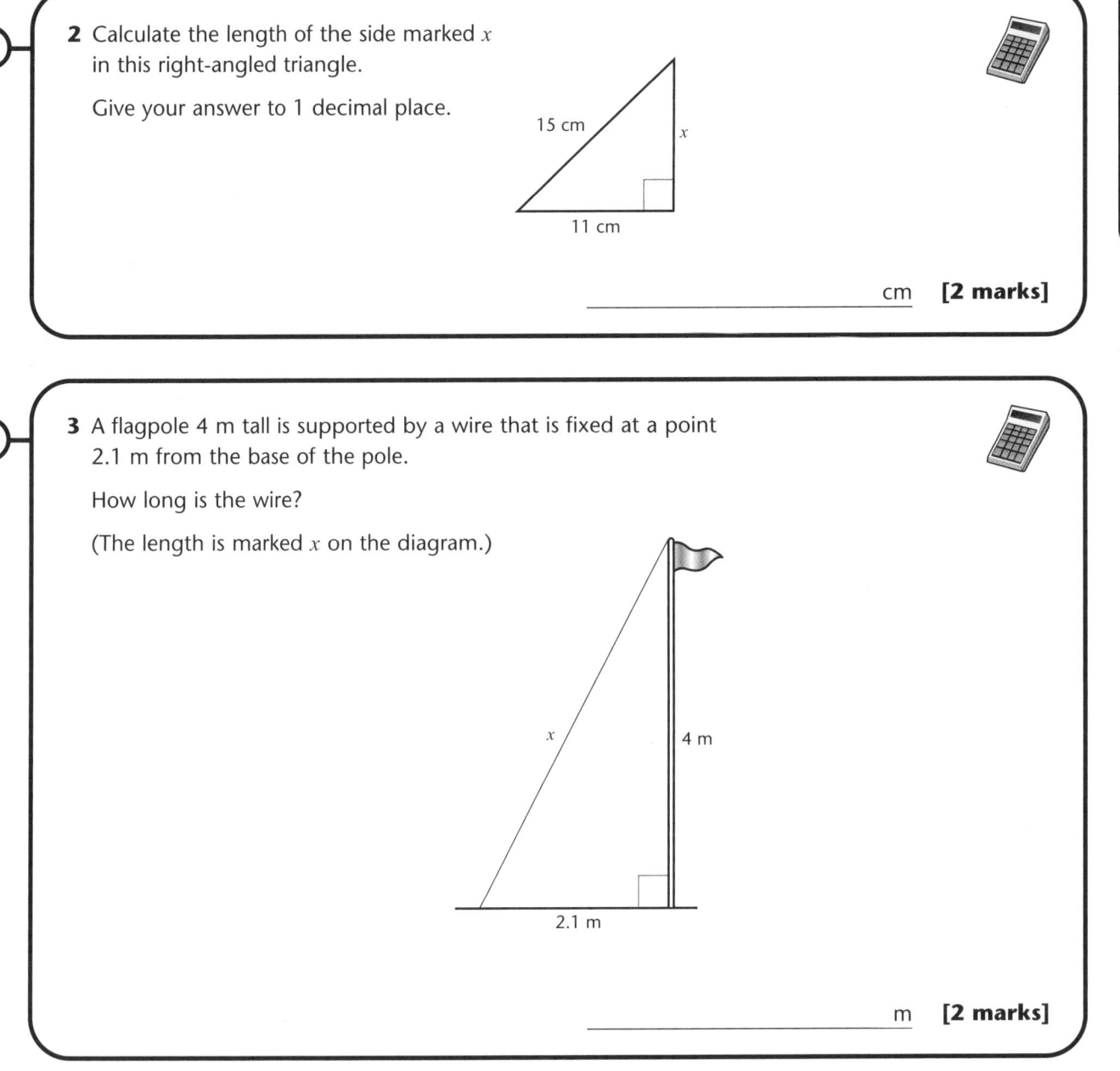

C

1 Calculate the length of the side marked x in this right-angled triangle.

Give your answer to 1 decimal place.

x

8 cm

10 cm

_____ cm **[2 marks]**

C

2 Calculate the length of the side marked x in this right-angled triangle.

Give your answer to 1 decimal place.

15 cm

x

11 cm

_____ cm **[2 marks]**

C

3 A flagpole 4 m tall is supported by a wire that is fixed at a point 2.1 m from the base of the pole.

How long is the wire?

(The length is marked x on the diagram.)

x

4 m

2.1 m

_____ m **[2 marks]**

This page tests you on
- Pythagoras' theorem • finding lengths of sides
- real-life problems

Shape, space and measures checklist

I can...

- ☐ find the perimeter of a 2-D shape
- ☐ find the area of a 2-D shape by counting squares
- ☐ draw lines of symmetry on basic 2-D shapes
- ☐ use the basic terminology associated with circles
- ☐ draw circles with a given radius
- ☐ recognise the net of a simple shape
- ☐ name basic 3-D solids
- ☐ recognise congruent shapes
- ☐ find the volume of a 3-D shape by counting squares

You are working at ⬭ Grade G ⬭ level.

- ☐ find the area of a rectangle, using the formula $A = lw$
- ☐ find the order of rotational symmetry for basic 2-D shapes
- ☐ measure and draw angles accurately
- ☐ use the facts that the angles on a straight line add up to 180° and the angles around a point add up to 360°
- ☐ draw and measure lines accurately
- ☐ draw the net of a simple 3-D shape
- ☐ read scales with a variety of divisions
- ☐ find the surface area of a 2-D shape by counting squares

You are working at ⬭ Grade F ⬭ level.

- ☐ find the area of a triangle using the formula $A = \frac{1}{2}bh$
- ☐ draw lines of symmetry on more complex 2-D shapes
- ☐ find the order of rotational symmetry for more complex 2-D shapes
- ☐ measure and draw bearings
- ☐ use the facts that the angles in a triangle add up to 180° and the angles in a quadrilateral add up to 360°
- ☐ find the exterior angle of a triangle and a quadrilateral
- ☐ recognise and find opposite angles
- ☐ draw simple shapes on an isometric grid
- ☐ tessellate a simple 2-D shape
- ☐ reflect a shape in the x- and y-axes
- ☐ convert from one metric unit to another
- ☐ convert from one imperial unit to another, given the conversion factor
- ☐ use the formula $V = lwh$ to find the volume of a cuboid
- ☐ find the surface area of a cuboid

You are working at ⬭ Grade E ⬭ level.

- ☐ find the area of a parallelogram, using the formula $A = bh$
- ☐ find the area of a trapezium, using the formula $\frac{1}{2}(a + b)h$
- ☐ find the area of a compound shape

- [ ] work out the formula for the perimeter, area or volume of simple shapes
- [ ] identify the planes of symmetry for 3-D shapes
- [ ] recognise and find alternate angles in parallel lines and a transversal
- [ ] recognise and find corresponding angles in parallel lines and a transversal
- [ ] recognise and find interior angles in parallel lines and a transversal
- [ ] use and recognise the properties of quadrilaterals
- [ ] find the exterior and interior angles of regular polygons
- [ ] understand the words 'sector' and 'segment' when used with circles
- [ ] calculate the circumference of a circle, giving the answer in terms of π if necessary
- [ ] calculate the area of a circle, giving the answer in terms of π if necessary
- [ ] recognise plan and elevation from isometric and other 3-D drawings
- [ ] translate a 2-D shape
- [ ] reflect a 2-D shape in lines of the form $y = a$, $x = b$
- [ ] rotate a 2-D shape about the origin
- [ ] enlarge a 2-D shape by a whole-number scale factor about the origin
- [ ] construct diagrams accurately, using compasses, a protractor and a straight edge
- [ ] use the appropriate conversion factors to change imperial units to metric units and vice versa

You are working at (**Grade D**) level.

- [ ] work out the formula for the perimeter, area or volume of complex shapes
- [ ] work out whether an expression or formula represents a length, an area or a volume
- [ ] relate the exterior and interior angles in regular polygons to the number of sides
- [ ] find the area and perimeter of semicircles
- [ ] translate a 2-D shape, using a vector
- [ ] reflect a 2-D shape in the lines $y = x$, $y = -x$
- [ ] rotate a 2-D shape about any point
- [ ] enlarge a 2-D shape by a fractional scale factor
- [ ] enlarge a 2-D shape about any centre
- [ ] construct perpendicular and angle bisectors
- [ ] construct an angle of 60°
- [ ] construct the perpendicular to a line from a point on the line and a point to a line
- [ ] draw simple loci
- [ ] work out the surface area and volume of a prism
- [ ] work out the volume of a cylinder, using the formula $V = \pi r^2 h$
- [ ] find the density of a 3-D shape
- [ ] find the hypotenuse of a right-angled triangle, using Pythagoras' theorem
- [ ] find the short side of a right-angled triangle, using Pythagoras' theorem
- [ ] use Pythagoras' theorem to solve real-life problems

You are working at (**Grade C**) level.

Basic algebra

1 The MacDonald family are Dad, Mum, Alfie and Bernice.

Alfie is x years old.

a Bernice is two years younger than Alfie.

Write down an expression for Bernice's age, in terms of x.

_____ **[1 mark]**

b Dad is twice as old as Alfie.

Write down an expression for Dad's age, in terms of x.

_____ **[1 mark]**

c Mum is twice Bernice's age.

Write down an expression for Mum's age, in terms of x.

_____ **[1 mark]**

d Write down and simplify an expression for the total age of the family, in terms of x.

_____ **[2 marks]**

2 a Draw lines to show which algebraic expressions are equivalent.

One line has been drawn for you.

	$3y$
$3y \times y$	$4y$
$3y + y$	$3y + 3$
$2y + y$	$5y + 2$
$3(y + 1)$	y^2
	$3y^2$

[3 marks]

b Simplify each of these expressions.

i $q + 4q - 2q$

_____ **[1 mark]**

ii $3p \times 5q$

_____ **[1 mark]**

iii $4x + 3 + 5x - 7$

_____ **[1 mark]**

This page tests you on • the language of algebra • simplifying expressions • collecting like terms • multiplying expressions

Expanding and factorising

1 a Expand $5(x - 3)$.

_____ **[1 mark]**

b Expand and simplify $2(x + 1) + 2(3x + 2)$.

_____ **[2 marks]**

c A rectangle has length $2x + 3$ and width $x + 3$.

Write down and simplify an expression for the perimeter, in terms of x.

$x + 3$

$2x + 3$

_____ **[2 marks]**

2 a Multiply out and simplify $3(x - 4) + 2(4x + 1)$.

_____ **[2 marks]**

b Factorise each expression.

i $4x + 6$ **ii** $5x^2 + 2x$

_____   _____ **[1 mark each]**

3 a Expand and simplify each expression.

i $2x(3x - 4y) - x(x + 3y)$

_____ **[1 mark]**

ii $6(2x - 3y) - 2(x - 3y)$

_____ **[1 mark]**

b Complete these factorisations.

i $3xy^2 + 6x^2y = 3xy(\_\_\_ + \_\_\_)$ **ii** $4ab^2 - 8a^2b + 2a^2b^2$
$= 2ab(\_\_\_ - \_\_\_ + \_\_\_)$ **[1 mark each]**

c Factorise fully $3p^2q^2 + 6pq$.

_____ **[1 mark]**

This page tests you on   • expanding brackets   • expand and simplify
                          • factorising

Quadratic expansion and substitution

1 a Expand $3(x + 2)$.

_____ **[1 mark]**

b Expand $x(x + 2)$.

_____ **[1 mark]**

c Expand and simplify $(x - 3)(x + 2)$.

_____ **[2 marks]**

d A rectangle has length $x + 2$ and width $x + 1$.

Write down an expression for the area, in terms of x, and simplify it.

$x + 1$

$x + 2$

_____ **[2 marks]**

C

2 a Multiply out and simplify $(x - 4)(x + 1)$.

_____ **[2 marks]**

b Multiply out and simplify $(x + 4)^2$.

_____ **[2 marks]**

C

3 a Work out the value of $3p + 2q$ when $p = -2$ and $q = 5$.

_____ **[1 mark]**

b Find the value of $a^2 + b^2$ when $a = 4$ and $b = 6$.

_____ **[1 mark]**

c An aeroplane has f first-class seats and e economy seats.

For a flight, each first-class seat costs £200 and each economy seat costs £50.

i If all seats are taken, write down an expression in terms of f and e for the total cost of all the seats in the aeroplane.

_____ **[1 mark]**

ii If $f = 20$ and $e = 120$, work out the actual cost of all the seats.

_____ **[1 mark]**

E

This page tests you on • quadratic expansion • squaring brackets • substitution

Linear equations

1 Solve these equations.

a $\dfrac{x}{3} + 5 = 4$

$x =$ _____ **[1 mark]**

b $3x + 4 = 1$

$x =$ _____ **[2 marks]**

c $\dfrac{7x - 2}{3} = 4$

$x =$ _____ **[2 marks]**

2 ABCD is a rectangle.

A ——— $x + 6$ ——— B

$3(y - 2)$ $y + 5$

D ——— $2x + 5$ ——— C

a Find the value of x.

$x =$ _____ **[2 marks]**

b Find the value of y.

$y =$ _____ **[2 marks]**

3 a Solve the equation $2x - 7 = 9$.

$x =$ _____ **[1 mark]**

b The solution to the equation $2x + 5 = 8$ is $x = 1\frac{1}{2}$.

Zoe thinks that the solution to $2(x + 5) = 8$ is also $x = 1\frac{1}{2}$.

Explain why Zoe is wrong.

_____

_____ **[1 mark]**

This page tests you on   • solving linear equations

1 a I think of a number, multiply it by 3 and add 5. The answer is 26.

  i Set up an equation to describe this.

  _____ **[1 mark]**

  ii Solve your equation to find the number.

  _____ **[1 mark]**

 b Solve these equations.

  i $4(3y - 2) = 16$

  $y =$ _____ **[2 marks]**

  ii $5x - 2 = x + 10$

  $x =$ _____ **[2 marks]**

2 Solve these equations.

 a $5x - 2 = 3x + 1$

  $x =$ _____ **[2 marks]**

 b $3(x + 4) = x - 5$

  $x =$ _____ **[2 marks]**

 c $5(x - 2) = 2(x + 4)$

  $x =$ _____ **[2 marks]**

3 Solve these equations.

 a $4(x + 3) = x + 3$

  $x =$ _____ **[2 marks]**

 b $5(2x - 1) = 2(x - 3)$

  $x =$ _____ **[2 marks]**

This page tests you on
- **solving equations with brackets**
- **equations with the variable on both sides of the equals sign**
- **equations with brackets and the variable on both sides**

E

1 a In the table, a, b, c and d each represent a different number.

The total of each row is shown at the side of the table.

a	a	a	a	16
a	a	b	b	20
a	a	b	c	21
a	b	c	d	25

Find the values of a, b, c and d.

$a =$ _____

$b =$ _____

$c =$ _____

$d =$ _____ **[2 marks]**

b i Write down an expression for the cost of x ice-lollies at 50p each and two choc-ices at 70p each.

_____ **[1 mark]**

ii The total cost of the x lollies and the two ice-lollies is £3.40.

Work out the value of x.

$x =$ _____ **[2 marks]**

C

2 The triangle has sides, given in centimetres, of x, $3x - 1$ and $2x + 5$.

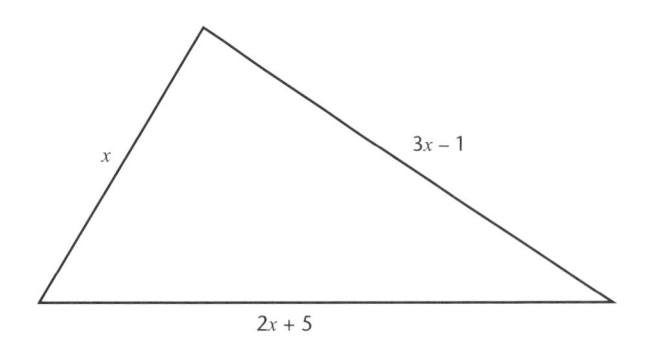

The perimeter of the triangle is 25 cm.

Find the value of x.

$x =$ _____ **[3 marks]**

This page tests you on • **setting up equations**

Trial and improvement

1 Use trial and improvement to solve the equation $x^3 + 4x = 203$.

The first two entries of the table are filled in.
Complete the table to find the solution.

Give your answer to 1 decimal place.

Guess	$x^3 + 4x$	Comment
5	145	Too low
6	240	Too high

$x =$ _____ **[3 marks]**

2 Darlene is using trial and improvement to find a solution to

$$2x + \frac{2}{x} = 8$$

The table shows her first trial.
Complete the table to find the solution.

Give your answer to 1 decimal place

Guess	$2x + \dfrac{2}{x}$	Comment
3	6.66	Too low

$x =$ _____ **[4 marks]**

This page tests you on • trial and improvement

Formulae

1 A widget weighs x grams.

A whotsit weighs 6 grams more than a widget.

a Write down an expression, in terms of x, for the weight of a whotsit.

_____ grams **[1 mark]**

b Write down an expression, in terms of x, for the total weight of three widgets and one whotsit.

_____ grams **[1 mark]**

c The total weight of three widgets and one whotsit is 27 grams.

Work out the weight of a widget.

_____ grams **[2 marks]**

2 a Explain why $5n - n \equiv 4n$ is an identity.

_____

_____ **[1 mark]**

b Explain why the equation $5(x + 1) - (x + 1) = 4(x + 1)$ does not have a solution.

_____

_____ **[1 mark]**

3 Rearrange each of these formulae to make x the subject.

a $C = \pi x$

$x =$ _____ **[1 mark]**

b $6y = 3x - 9$

Simplify your answer as much as possible.

$x =$ _____ **[2 marks]**

This page tests you on • formulae, identities, expressions and equations
• rearranging formulae

Inequalities

1 a Solve the inequality: $3x - 4 \leqslant 2$.

_____ **[1 mark]**

b What inequality is shown on the number line?

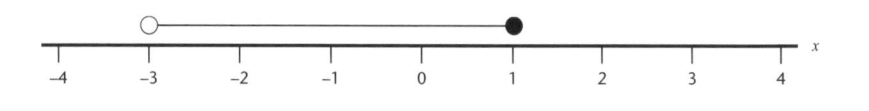

-4 -3 -2 -1 0 1 2 3 4 x

_____ **[1 mark]**

c Write down all the integers that satisfy both inequalities in parts **a** and **b**.

_____ **[1 mark]**

2 a What inequality is shown on the number line?

-4 -3 -2 -1 0 1 2 3 4 x

_____ **[1 mark]**

b Solve these inequalities.

i $\dfrac{x}{2} + 3 > 1$

_____ **[2 marks]**

ii $\dfrac{x + 3}{2} \leqslant 1$

_____ **[2 marks]**

c What integers satisfy both of the inequalities in parts **a** and **b**?

_____ **[1 mark]**

This page tests you on • inequalities • solving inequalities
• inequalities on number lines

Graphs

1 This is a conversion graph between miles and kilometres.

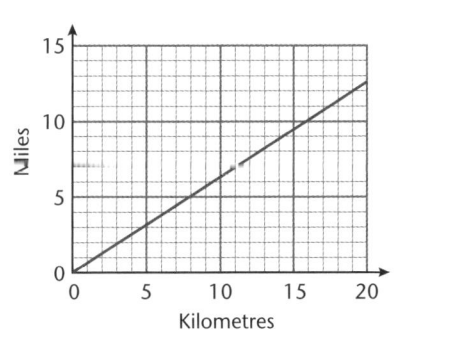

a Approximately how many miles is 5 kilometres? _____ miles **[1 mark]**

b Approximately how many kilometres is 8 miles? _____ km **[1 mark]**

c Use the graph to work out how many miles is equivalent to 160 kilometres.

_____ miles **[1 mark]**

2 Martin does a walk from his house to a viewpoint, 5 kilometres from his house and back again.

The distance–time graph shows his journey.

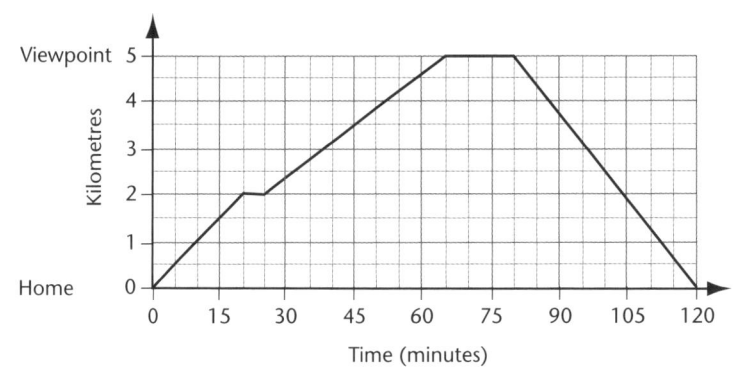

a The viewpoint is uphill from Martin's house.

Martin takes a rest before walking up the steepest part of the hill.

i How far from home was Martin when he took a rest?

_____ km **[1 mark]**

ii How long did Martin rest? _____ minutes **[1 mark]**

b Martin stopped at the viewpoint before returning home.

He then walked quickly home at a steady pace.

i How long did it take Martin to return home? _____ minutes **[1 mark]**

ii What was Martin's average speed on the way home?

_____ km/h **[1 mark]**

Linear graphs

1 The table shows some values of the function $y = 3x + 1$ for values of x from –1 to 3.

a Complete the table of values.

x	–1	0	1	2	3
y	–2				10

[1 mark]

b Use the table to draw the graph of $y = 3x + 1$.

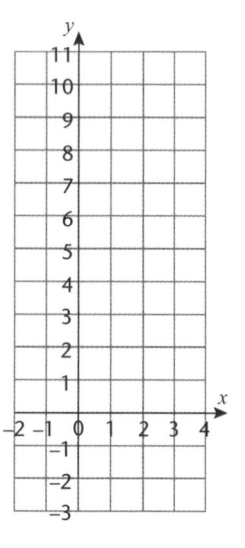

[2 marks]

c What is the x-value when $y = 8$? _____ **[1 mark]**

2 Draw the graph of $y = 2x - 1$ for $-3 \leqslant x \leqslant 3$.

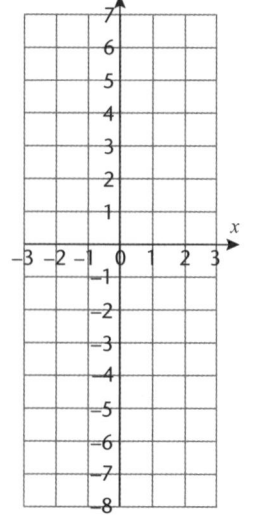

[2 marks]

This page tests you on • negative coordinates • drawing graphs from tables
• drawing linear graphs

1 Here are the equations of six lines.

A: $y = 3x + 6$ B: $y = 2x - 1$ C: $y = \dfrac{x}{2} - 1$

D: $y = 3x + 1$ E: $y = \dfrac{x}{3} + 1$ F: $y = 4x + 2$

a Which line is parallel to line A?

_____   **[1 mark]**

b Which line crosses the y-axis at the same point as line B?

_____   **[1 mark]**

c Which other two lines intersect on the y-axis?

_____   **[1 mark]**

d Write down the gradient of each of these lines.

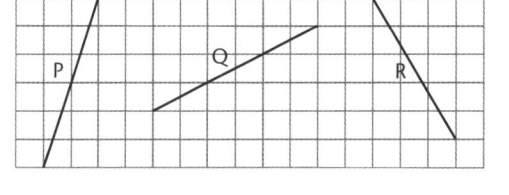

Line P _____   Line Q _____   Line R _____   **[3 marks]**

2 Use the gradient-intercept method to draw the graph of $y = 3x - 2$ for $-3 \leqslant x \leqslant 3$.

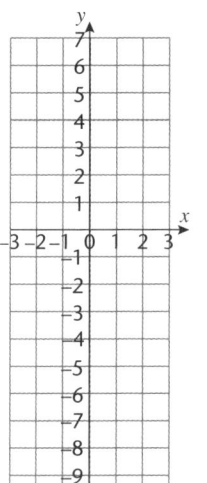

[2 marks]

This page tests you on   • gradients • the gradient–intercept method
• drawing a line with a given gradient

Quadratic graphs

1 a Complete the table of values for the graph of $y = x^2 + 3$.

x	−3	−2	−1	0	1	2	3
y	12	7					12

[1 mark]

b Draw the graph of $y = x^2 + 3$ for values of x from −3 to 3.

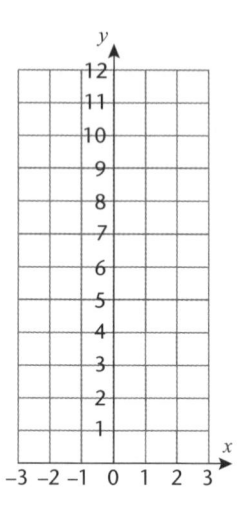

[2 marks]

2 a Complete the table of values for the graph of $y = x^2 − 3x − 4$.

x	−2	−1	0	1	2	3	4
y	6	0			−6		0

[1 mark]

b Draw the graph of $y = x^2 − 3x − 4$ for values of x from −2 to 4.

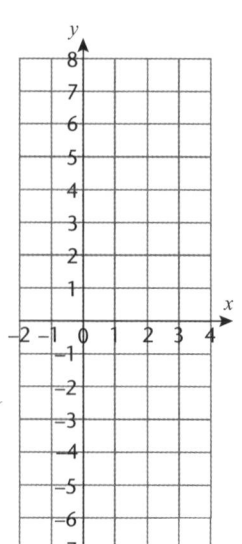

[2 marks]

This page tests you on • drawing quadratic graphs

C

1 a Complete the table of values for the graph of $y = x^2 - 2x + 1$.

x	-2	-1	0	1	2	3	4
y	9	4	1				

[1 mark]

b Draw the graph of $y = x^2 - 2x + 1$
for values of x from -2 to 4.

[2 marks]

c Use the graph to find the x-values when $y = 6$. _____ [1 mark]

d Use the graph to solve the equation $x^2 - 2x + 1 = 0$.

_____ [1 mark]

C

2 a Complete the table of values for the graph of $y = x^2 + 2x - 1$.

x	-4	-3	-2	-1	0	1	2
y		2	-1				7

[1 mark]

b Draw the graph of $y = x^2 + 2x - 1$
for values of x from -4 to 2.

[2 marks]

c Use the graph to find the x-values when $y = 1.5$. _____ [1 mark]

d Use the graph to solve the equation $x^2 + 2x - 1 = 0$.

_____ [1 mark]

This page tests you on
• reading values from quadratic graphs
• using graphs to solve quadratic equations

Pattern

1 a Here are three lines of a series of number calculations.

$$1 = 1 = 1^2$$
$$1 + 3 = 4 = 2^2$$
$$1 + 3 + 5 = 9 = 3^2$$
$$\underline{\hspace{1cm}} = \underline{\hspace{1cm}} = \underline{\hspace{1cm}}$$
$$\underline{\hspace{1cm}} = \underline{\hspace{1cm}} = \underline{\hspace{1cm}}$$

Complete the next two lines of the pattern.　　**[2 marks]**

b 1, 3, 5, 7, 9, 11, ... are the **odd numbers**.

What is the 50th odd number?

_____　**[1 mark]**

c 1, 4, 9, ... are the **square numbers**.

What is the 15th square number?

_____　**[1 mark]**

2 Squares are used to make patterns.

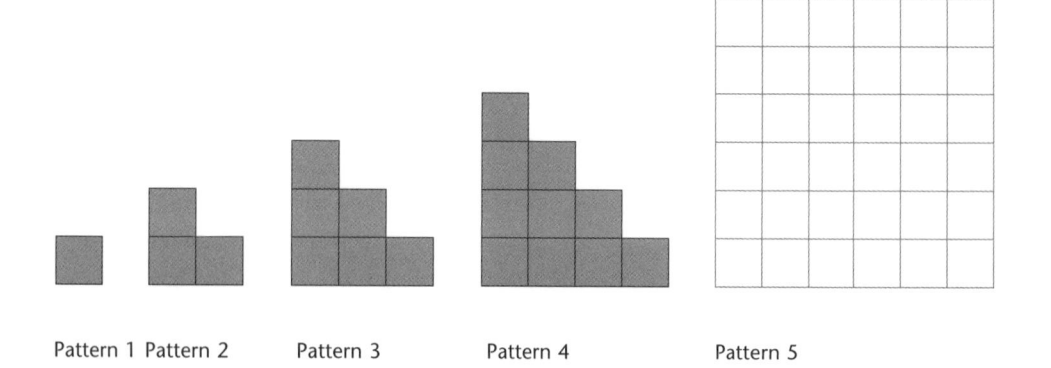

Pattern 1　Pattern 2　　　Pattern 3　　　　Pattern 4　　　　Pattern 5

a Draw pattern 5.　　**[1 mark]**

b Complete the table that shows the number of squares in each pattern.

Pattern number	1	2	3	4	5
Number of squares	1	3			

[2 marks]

c Describe, in words, the rule for continuing the number of squares.

_____

_____　**[1 mark]**

This page tests you on　　• patterns in number　• number sequences

The *n*th term

C

1 The *n*th term of a sequence is $4n + 1$.

  a Write down the first three terms of the sequence.

  [1 mark]

  b Which term of the sequence is equal to 29?

  [1 mark]

  c Explain why 84 is not a term in this sequence.

  [1 mark]

  d What is the *n*th term of the sequence 3, 10, 17, 24, 31, ___?

  [2 marks]

C

2 Matches are used to make patterns with hexagons.

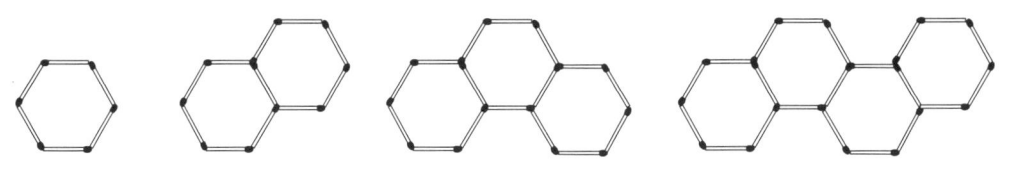

Pattern 1   Pattern 2   Pattern 3   Pattern 4

  a Complete the table that shows the number of matches used to make each pattern.

Pattern number	1	2	3	4	5
Number of squares	6	11			

  [2 marks]

  b How many matches will be needed to make the 20th pattern?

  [1 mark]

  c How many matches will be needed to make the *n*th pattern?

  [2 marks]

Sequences

1 R is an odd number, Q is an even number, P is a prime number.

State whether these expressions are *always even*, *always odd* or *could be either*.

	Always even	**Always odd**	**Could be either**	
a $R + Q$	☐	☐	☐	[1 mark]
b RQ	☐	☐	☐	[1 mark]
c $P + Q$	☐	☐	☐	[1 mark]
d R^2	☐	☐	☐	[1 mark]
e $R + PQ$	☐	☐	☐	[1 mark]

D

2 a n is a positive integer.

Explain why $2n$ is always an even number.

_____

_____ [1 mark]

b Zoe says that when you square an even number you always get a multiple of 4.

Show that Zoe is correct.

_____

_____ [2 marks]

C

3 Triangles are used to make patterns.

 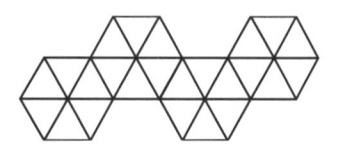

Pattern 1   Pattern 2   Pattern 3

a Complete the table that shows the number of triangles used to make each pattern.

Pattern number	1	2	3	4	5
Number of triangles	12				

[2 marks]

b How many triangles will be needed to make the nth pattern?

_____ [2 marks]

E

This page tests you on
• special sequences
• finding the nth term from given patterns

Algebra checklist

I can...

- [ ] use a formula expressed in words
- [ ] substitute numbers into expressions
- [ ] use letters to write a simple algebraic expression
- [ ] solve linear equations that require only one inverse operation to solve
- [ ] read values from a conversion graph
- [ ] plot coordinates in all four quadrants
- [ ] give the next value in a linear sequence
- [ ] describe how a linear sequence is building up

You are working at (Grade F) level.

- [ ] simplify an expression by collecting like terms
- [ ] simplify expressions by multiplying terms
- [ ] solve linear equations that require more than one inverse operation to solve
- [ ] read distances and times from a travel graph
- [ ] draw a linear graph from a table of values
- [ ] find any number term in a linear sequence
- [ ] recognise patterns in number calculations

You are working at (Grade E) level.

- [ ] use letters to write more complicated algebraic expressions
- [ ] expand expressions with brackets
- [ ] factorise simple expressions
- [ ] solve linear equations where the variable appears on both sides of the equals sign
- [ ] solve linear equations that require the expansion of a bracket
- [ ] set up and solve simple equations from real-life situations
- [ ] find the average speed from a travel graph
- [ ] draw a linear graph without a table of values
- [ ] substitute numbers into an nth term rule
- [ ] understand how odd and even numbers interact in addition, subtraction and multiplication problems

You are working at (Grade D) level.

- [ ] expand and simplify expressions involving brackets
- [ ] factorise expressions involving letters and numbers
- [ ] expand pairs of linear brackets to give a quadratic expression
- [ ] solve linear equations that have the variable on both sides and include brackets
- [ ] solve simple linear inequalities
- [ ] show inequalities on a number line
- [ ] solve equations, using trial and improvement
- [ ] rearrange simple formulae
- [ ] use a table of values to draw a simple quadratic graph
- [ ] use a table of values to draw a more complex quadratic graph
- [ ] solve a quadratic equation from a graph
- [ ] give the nth term of a linear sequence
- [ ] give the nth term of a sequence of powers of 2 or 10.

You are working at (Grade C) level.

Formulae sheet

Area of trapezium $= \frac{1}{2}(a + b)h$

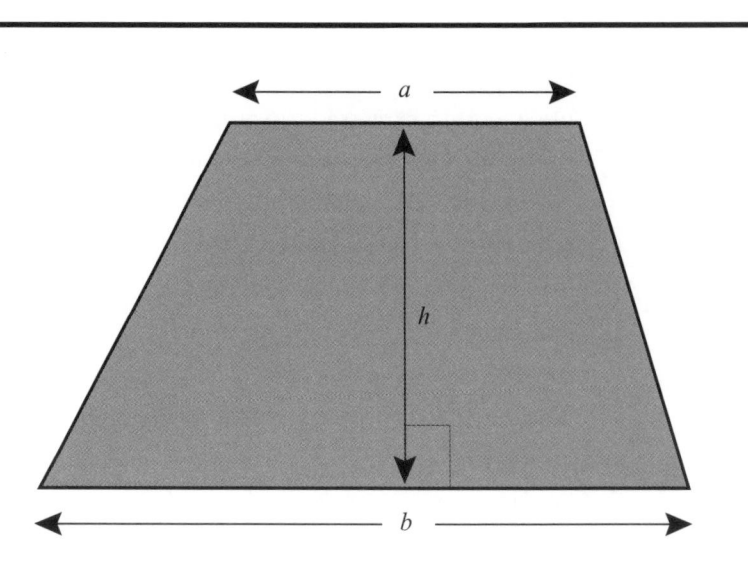

Volume of prism = acrea of cross-section × length

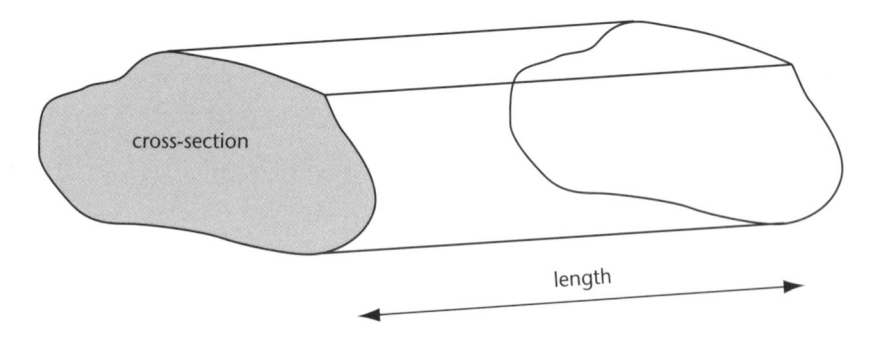